Conversations with a Hungry Ghost

Memoir of a Reluctant Medium

CAROLE LOUIE

Join the conversation at carolelouie.com

Red Thread of Fate Publishing

ISBN#978-0-9988334-0-8

TO

Jennie, David, Jake, and Marisa

With love

Genealogy Chart from Louie Fat

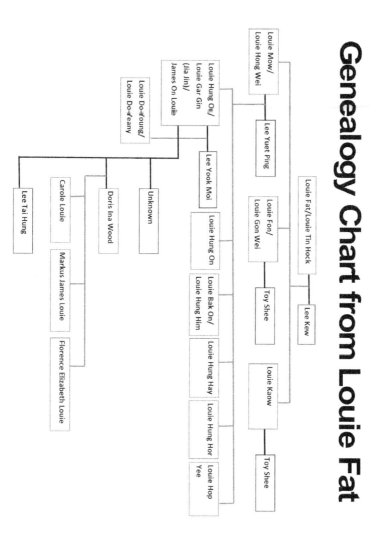

Table of Contents

Introduction

DIVINE ORDER

2017
Richmond, Virginia

Why did it take so long for me to accept my gift as a medium? If only I'd known that by trusting in my Higher Self, I'd discover the key to healing the past, I would have surrendered sooner. If only I'd known that life is not only a journey but also a process, I would have known everything is in Divine Order.

It doesn't matter that it took me a quarter of a century or the unusual path that guided me to the truth about my past because I am on a unique spiritual journey. I hope by sharing my story, you will gain insight into your process, especially if you've ever seen a ghost, been abused, or wondered about the skeletons in your family's closet. Like me, you might discover their interconnections.

It was challenging at times to stay focused on current circumstances when the memories haunted me and pulled me back to the traumatic events that led up to the day we ran away from my father.

As anyone who has struggled with Post Traumatic Stress Disorder will tell you, the oddest smell or sound can trigger a spontaneous flashback. For me, a tone of a person's voice caused me to freeze in fear and hold my breath, unable to function. The pungent smell of Tiger Balm Ointment over thirty years after Dad molested me made me want to run out of the room again. Life is not like the big screen where stories unfold in two hours, but our Higher Self or Soul knows when we are ready to tackle the issues that hold us back from our spiritual growth.

My evolution not only meant healing the wounds from my childhood but also accepting my gift as a medium and learning how to resolve unfinished issues from previous lives. These aspects were as interwoven as the inner and outer rings of a spider's web. I brushed the hints about patterns of my life aside as one would a cobweb. I ignored the ghosts who stood by my bed even when they poked me with icy cold fingers.

***

Sitting around my grandmother's wood burning stove sipping sassafras tea when I lived with my grandparents in 1959, I asked Grannie about the people who walked through her house late at night.

She said, "Oh, they's just my relatives who forgets which room I'm in. Don't pay them no nevermind and iffin they scare you, just tell them *God go between me and thee.*"

***

It comforted me that my grandmother saw ghosts and received messages from them, but not enough that I accepted the spirits who followed me wherever I lived.

An experience with a Ouija board when I was seventeen didn't help alleviate my fears. My friend Peggy and I played on her board until one night as we waited for a message to slowly reveal itself, I lost interest and allowed my attention to drift to the television in the other room. I turned back to the board when Peggy and my sister screamed. We watched as my hand levitated over the Ouija board and pulled me toward the enclosed staircase. I felt I'd die if I moved in that direction. We ended the session, and I went home, but I could not sleep without the light on, the covers up to my chin, and my Bible on my chest.

Working in the library at college the next year, I discovered the occult section and a book about palmistry. I'd play at reading people's palms, but I doubted myself until I was able to validate the details.

I did not take the readings seriously until 1987 when I read a friend's hand at a party. I began to cry. I felt sadness in her home, but that was all I could see. A few months later her partner died, and my friend avoided me as if I were a leper.

Feeling unsettled by this experience, I shut down. However, when my father died in 1990, and I saw his etheric body standing near Auntie Tai, his common-law wife, at his funeral, I knew it was time to overcome my fear of ghosts.

Even though his etheric body was like a mirage, I saw the sleeve of his favorite suit, the veins that bulged in his hand, and the red stone in his Masonic ring before the image evaporated.

My clenched jaw and shallow breathing showed me that I was as afraid of his ghost as I was of him when I was a child.

It was too much to process during the funeral.

After years of suppressing my feelings, all I could do was scream silently. Rather than dwell in chaos, I decided to channel my energies into overcoming my fear of ghosts. This decision was my first step toward accepting my gift as a blessing instead of a curse.

When I embraced this aspect about me, I faced a challenge of what to do. My teacher encouraged me to become a professional psychic; however, that did not feel right. During meditation, I had a vision of utilizing my gifts to heal, and even though I did not know how, I knew that the first person I needed to focus on was myself.

I had no idea in the beginning that learning to speak with ghosts was the first of many steps on my spiritual path that led me to a bigger picture about the evolution of humankind, to an understanding that we are all on a spiritual path.

Just because you are on a spiritual path does not mean that you will encounter ghosts, but I hope my story will help you become aware of those things that hold you back from life.

Even though my book centers on my Chinese heritage, it is about the connections we all experience. Rooting for my ancestors became the gateway to my spiritual awakening.

A note about the Chinese names in the book: Chinese use the last name first to honor their family lineage. Therefore, my father's name was Louie Hung On when he was born. When he married, his married name was Louie Gar Gin. His American name was James On Louie. However, I recently met one of his cousins, a man in his eighties, who did not recognize my father until I said Dad's birth name.

The transliteration system (method of translating Chinese characters into a Romanized form) used by the immigration officials varied from one interpreter to another; and the early translators did not always conform to the Wade-Giles system, which is different from the current pinyin system.

My half-brother's name was Louie Do-Young, which meant that our grandfather raised him. When he came to the United States, Do-Young changed the spelling to Do-Yeany, which means "second chance." (I hyphenated his name to avoid grammar issues.)

Chinese names can be confusing. I used the names that I was familiar with regardless of the transliteration. Therefore, I included genealogy charts from my great-grandfather to my generation as a guide.

Let's begin where I first communicated with my father's ghost in the Tenth Hell of the Buddha.

Chapter 1

BECOMING A MEDIUM

1992
Naples, Florida

Here I go again. A familiar tug at my third eye, a tingling sensation spread from my forehead pressing against my eye sockets and down to my upper lip as the music of Tibetan Buddhist monks chanting filled the meditation room. My spirit rose above my body as the veil between the meditation circle and the Tenth Hell of the Buddha disappeared. Before I could question what I saw in my mind's eye, the music pulled me deeper and deeper until I felt as if I'd slipped through Alice in Wonderland's rabbit hole.

***

My vision blurred around the edges, but before me, an intricately carved kang sat in an alcove adorned with painted panels depicting the seasons.

Butterflies danced around the white peonies of spring, followed by ducks swimming by the white lotus blossoms that heralded summer. Balls of white chrysanthemums announced fall's arrival while white plum blossoms created lacy patterns against a winter sky.

A Buddha-like man sat crossed legged on silk brocade cushions of saffron and maroon on the wooden kang used as a sofa or a bed. He propped his left elbow on a pile of pillows at his side, and his right arm rested on the scholar's table that filled the middle of the kang during the day. Embroidered silk slippers sat at the ready on the saffron and maroon, wool and silk rug that had a classic shou/longevity medallion in the middle. Eight Taoist symbols of immortality adorned the rug's border. Incense from bronze tripod incense burners strategically placed on each side of the kang wafted about him.

I recognized the man who sat folded up into a ball at the foot of the kang's platform. I saw his white chef's jacket pulled down exposing his flimsy undershirt. He sobbed as he pulled at his hair and slapped his exposed bony shoulders. Sweat dripped from his hairline and followed the curve of his back. He lifted his head. If I entertained any doubts before, they melted away when I saw my father's face.

"Lord Buddha," Dad said. "I am ashamed. I know what I did wrong."

Looking around at the others who writhed in agony in their corners of this hell, he knew his sins had caught up with him. "Will I be in the Tenth Hell forever?"

Free-standing banners in Chinese calligraphy described each person's sin. I turned to get a wider view of the people around him. I could not sense the cause of their torment, but I knew my father's.

"What can do? I watched Calo cry. I felt her suffering. What I did wrong." He sighed. "Will I always be a hungry ghost in this hell forever, to be released only once a year during the Festival of the Hungry Ghost?"

What I saw was not what I expected of Hell. No fire and brimstone. No devil with a pitchfork, images conjured up from my mother's Southern Baptist roots, but maybe Christian Hell and Buddhist Hell are different. What is Hell, after all? I had a feeling I was going to find out. My body floated upward to get a better view, but a fog prevented me from seeing anything other than my father and the Buddha. Effortlessly, I zoomed back in as incense spiraled upwards toward me.

Tucking in his maroon robe as he adjusted his position, the Buddha shifted one leg over the edge of the kang. His stocking feet barely touched the rug as he leaned forward to prop his elbows on his knee. He said, "Come closer, Jimmy."

Dad crawled up on the platform like a spider. "Closer," the Buddha murmured.

Dad prostrated at the Buddha's feet. "I will do anything you ask of me," he said.

"Anything?" the Buddha said.

Still uncertain as I meandered my way through this out-of-body experience, I wondered how was I able to sense whether the Buddha knew if Dad's intentions matched his words or not, and how did I?

"Anything," he replied bending lower, touching his forehead to the floor.

"Turn around and face the one you injured." The Buddha turned to where I stood and pointed at me.

I flinched. The Buddha sees me!

"Can you help your daughter overcome her fear of ghosts whether you will be free or not?" he asked tenderly yet firmly. A soft golden aura encompassed the Buddha's body, and I felt compassion radiating from him like the sun's rays lighting up the sky at sunrise touching my skin. Suddenly, I felt calm and peaceful.

Dad squinted. "But I am ashamed. How can I face her? She must hate me."

"Show her your shame. Do what you must do and do it now before it is too late."

Dad looked again in the direction the Buddha pointed. This time, Dad saw me. "Calo, that you? How you here? You forgive me?" Then, convulsive sobs overwhelmed him.

"I always wanted to forgive you," I said. I meant it. I reached out my hand but suddenly the Tenth Hell disappeared. I pulled back.

A stucco wall capped with a row of terra cotta tiles appeared. Somehow, I knew the wall surrounded a monastery.

Clusters of bamboo in blue and white porcelain pots with a dragon design flanked a massive eight-sided wooden door with a yin/yang medallion carved in the center. Four dragons amid arabesque vines circled the medallion.

A breeze rustled the bamboo creating a soft, welcoming sound like water dripping off the roof in a gentle rain. The door opened to a moon gate, an inner garden, and a line of monks dressed in saffron robes, carrying a brown robe which they draped over Dad's body. Then they walked with him through the doorway toward the inner garden beyond the moon gate and into the monastery.

Dad was free at last, no longer to roam as a hungry ghost, but how did I know this?

***

As if on cue, the music ended. I snapped back into my body sitting atop the carpeted floor. I pulled my blanket around me as I sat there and searched for a tissue to catch the tears streaming down my cheeks.

My friend Sunny, who sat next to me, sensed my distress, and put her earth mother arms around me. "Did you hear someone sobbing during the meditation?" she said.

"Oh, Sunny. Wait until I tell you what just happened." I moved my arms and legs slowly. I breathed deeply and scanned my body to be sure I was fully back. My body felt heavy like a boxer's punching bag.

If you'd asked me what a hungry ghost was in 1990, I would not have known what to tell you. That was the year Dad died. That was the year I questioned death.

Hungry ghosts? Tenth Hell? What had I gotten myself into? I could not undo what I had done. I could not pretend I did not see my father's ghost, did not hear his voice, and did not hear the Buddha's voice. *What happens now?* I thought, unsure if I meant what happens to Dad or what happens to me, or both.

After a lifetime of blocking out the ghosts that I saw as a child, I desperately wanted to know what my father's ghost had to say. Little did I suspect that he would finally understand why I wanted to know about my heritage.

In the past, when I had asked him to tell me about China, about Buddhism, and about his family, he'd flip his hand in the air as if to erase the question. He'd say, "You be American." I did not know then why that command was so important to him, but I do now because the conversations with him have taught me not only that hungry ghosts are more than lost souls, but also that they are hungry for love.

I flashed back to Dad's wake. I felt chills through my body. I looked around expecting to see Dad. I sat in silence, going through the motions of the wake and funeral. I jotted down notes and took photos like an investigative reporter because it wasn't every day that I attended a Buddhist funeral.

After Dad's funeral, I hoped that learning about Buddhist's beliefs about the afterlife would help me understand why ghosts had followed me all my life. However, I did not know any Buddhists in Naples, FL. So, I joined a meditation group and took metaphysical classes in search of how to talk to ghosts, at least, to my father's ghost. I wanted to know why I felt his anger at his funeral. Was Dad angry because we did not take the food to the cemetery? I remembered taking food to the gravesite at the first Buddhist funeral I went to as a child and my sister Florence getting her hands slapped because she tried to eat some of the rice. Or was it because Auntie Tai sat on the right side of the mortuary, the side reserved for friends?

I thought I was living a normal life. Normal for someone from a broken home, someone who survived sexual abuse, two divorces, and undiagnosed post-traumatic stress. I was a successful interior designer getting ready to start a new job with an elite design studio, but I also struggled in my third marriage. Then, my father died.

Although I tried to have a healthy relationship with Dad, I was not close to him. How could I be when memories about him molesting me, about my family running away from him when I was nine, and about our strange reunion when I was twenty-two haunted me? How could I have a normal relationship with him when he died without acknowledging what he did to my mother, our family, or me? He died without asking for forgiveness.

Remembering the same feelings when ghosts stood by my bedside, I shuddered uncontrollably. The tips of my ears tingled. My breathing became shallow. But this time, I knew who the ghost was, and this time, I wanted to talk. I wanted to hear what he had to say.

Learning to communicate with ghosts is a process. My process began by learning to calm my mind and the thoughts that raced from family to job, to design projects, and a million other distractions. I had to let go of my fear of ghosts conjured up by scary movies and ghoulish stories, fear that made me sleep with the lights on and the covers up to my chin. Meditation helped. In a relaxed state, I was receptive. Classes about channeling helped me to focus my attention like a laser on a different frequency. At first, the messages sounded like a garbled reception of a radio station. With practice, I heard the voices of spirits from the other side. Their primary message was "We are not dead." For me, that statement created a hundred questions about what happens in the afterlife.

Although raised as a Christian, I was open-minded about exploring other faiths because Christian teachings did not answer all my questions. My conversations with Dad caused my thinking about all religions to evolve.

Chapter 2

TRUTH CANNOT BE BURIED

May 12, 1990
San Francisco, California

I tossed the white ribbon that designated my position as a daughter onto the coffin. Sunlight broke through the clouds, creating a pattern of light and shadow on the copper top of the coffin dotted with pieces of black, green, and white fabric, pieces that identified the position of each family member from eldest son to youngest great-grandchild. Dad always said I brought the sunshine with me to San Francisco; if only I'd brought some warmth. The cold, Pacific wind blew over Colma-San Francisco's City of the Dead, known for its population of deceased residents who outnumbered the living. I surveyed the well-manicured grounds of the Woodlawn Cemetery, established by the Masons, in 1904 after San Francisco passed an ordinance to move all gravesites out of the city.

I looked back at the tombstone and the hillside dotted with granite markers. The place felt more like a country club than burial grounds.

Pulling my jacket tighter around me to protect me from the breeze that blew before the fog rolled in, I felt as if the world was moving in slow-motion.

What a waste! Who needs a castle entrance, an expensive coffin, granite headstone, fancy cemetery? Who needs elaborate funeral rituals and a marching band?

"Calo," Do-Yeany, my older brother said. He motioned to me to join the rest of the family, consisting of Chinese immigrants as well as three Amer-Asian offspring, and our children. As the family headed back to the funeral cars to a banquet in one of the family's restaurants, I replied, "I'm coming, Di Lo," calling him by the designation "older brother" that I learned the day before.

"Calo," Dad said as I turned with hesitation to leave. He looked down at the coffin and then reached out to touch my arm. "Why I here? This not what I planned," he snapped.

Feeling the familiar sensation that I knew from my childhood when ghosts poked me with their cold fingers, I jerked back. "You are here," I said, running my fingers over the top of Dad's tombstone, "I just know it. Why can't I talk to you?"

Goosebumps covered my body. I shuddered as the ugly memories tucked away long ago, somewhere in the recesses of my mind, reared up again.

Flashbacks ricocheted in my mind: a light glinting on a cleaver struck a chord of fear, the pungent smell of Tiger Balm ointment made me recoil, the rattle of a hand on the door threatened to invade my safety, cursing in a language I could not understand stirred my instinct to run and hide.

Fear tinged everything. It had followed me like a shadow my entire life. Dad's actions set up a chain of events like rows of karmic dominoes waiting to be tipped.

Dad called out to me again, "Calo." Frustrated, he pulled at his stray overgrown nose hairs. He spat on the ground and then, mumbled to himself the way he did whenever he smelled dog excrement on the sidewalk.

"I here, Calo," Dad said patting his chest. He looked down at the coffin and then at me. "I right here. I not down there," pointing to the coffin. "Aiya!"

Do-Yeany called again. I snapped back from that place I go to when lost in my thoughts. I knew I had to leave. I looked down at the coffin one last time. "Goodbye, Daddy," I whispered. "Talk to me. Please talk to me."

CAROLE LOUIE

Chapter 3

REUNION

June 1989
San Francisco, California

"We're here. Mark and Florence are with me," I said as the others—my brother and sister and our families—gathered around the phone in my room. I studied the expressions on their faces, then looked out the window towards the Coit Tower. The sky was a clear blue. Dad always said I brought the sunshine with me to San Francisco. He startled me with his reply.

"Don't come," Dad said, "Don't come. Too much money. Save your money."

"He doesn't understand," I said as I covered the phone with my hand. *It was not such a brilliant idea to surprise Dad.* I removed my hand and spoke in a louder voice, "We're here right now. We're coming over this afternoon, okay?" It was not a question, but I had to give him a sense of respect. I heard a deep sigh on the other end of the phone.

"Okay, Calo. You come."

I turned back to Mark and Florence and continued, "It was the only way. We are here now, and he will be glad we came as soon as we see him. This is one heck of a reunion."

"He'll get over it. It has been a long time. Let's go," Florence said as she quickly headed to the door and everyone followed on cue.

It was foolish to hope our reunion would erase the painful memory of Dad coming home to find an empty house in the summer of 1957. The day our mother packed us into the car and ran away from him. I will never forget the picture in my mind of Dad waiting for his young family to return. He sat at the table at the A & W Root Beer stand on Monterey Street in Gilroy, California. He watched every car pass by, hoping that our green and white '57 Chevy would return.

After all those years, we could come together. It was a time to put the past behind us, to pay our respects (filial piety), to our dying father.

Four generations gathered at my father's flat. The first generation included Dad and Auntie Tai, his companion or common-law wife. Although they lived together for many years, they never married. In old China, Auntie Tai was a "concubine".

The second generation (in chronological order)—*my generation*—consisted of my older half-brother, and the only child of my father's first wife, Do-Yeany and his wife, Yam Oy; me and my husband, Jon; my younger brother, Mark, and his wife, Abby; and my younger sister, Florence, and her husband, Bob.

The third generation (in chronological order) included Do-Yeany's oldest son, Wai Kim, and his wife, Wai Zhen; Do-Yeany's youngest son, Wai Gauy, and his wife, Shao Yun; Laura, Florence's daughter; and Jennie, my daughter.

The fourth generation (in chronological order) consisted of Wai Kim's daughter, Mabel, and Wai Gauy's sons, George, and Vincent.

When my father lived in China, it was common for four generations to live under the same roof or in the same compound. Things were different in the U.S. The Amer-Asian part of the family lived from one end of the United States to the other. While we grew up in the U.S., Do-Yeany and his family lived in China. They came to America in the late 1970's and early 1980's.

Dad and Auntie Tai lived in one of Dad's apartments, Do-Yeany and Yam Oy lived in another one in the same building. Do-Yeany's sons and their families lived in separate houses. They were becoming American in many ways.

While Chinese families get together for feasts on special occasions, this was the first time all of Dad's children gathered in one place.

I rang the doorbell and waited for the sound of footsteps on the steep stairwell. I heard Auntie Tai's familiar voice call out the bay window, "Calo! Calo!"

We entered, while Auntie Tai chattered at the top of the stairs and my grandnephews and grandniece ran around excitedly. Auntie Tai brought cups and a teapot to the front room and began serving tea. It was awkward at first, but the awkwardness gave way to laughter and joy.

I watched my elder brother sip his tea. Do-Yeany grew up in China, where his grandparents raised him after his mother died only a few days after Do-Yeany was born. Dad had returned to the United States, the gold mountain, before his son was born. He was charged with a mission to create prosperity for his family; but the struggle in China that led to the Japanese invasion, World War II, and the Communist take-over made it impossible for him to return. He began a new life in San Francisco, California.

Do-Yeany was in his late forties when he reunited with his father after relations opened between China and the United States. Dad brought Do-Yeany to San Francisco in 1979. Yam Oy, Do-Yeany's wife, and their sons followed. My nephews went back to China to marry the women they had committed to marry, and then they all came to the United States. Their children, born in San Francisco, are sometimes called "American Born Chinese" (ABC or Chinese Americans).

I wondered what their lives in China were like and what they might have been if Dad had returned to China instead of staying in the United States. I wondered why Dad did not tell me I had an older brother until I was sixteen years old.

When I read Dad's letter in 1964, I learned I not only had an older brother but also that he and his family lived in near poverty in Communist China. I was so over-whelmed by the letter that I wrote a speech about Do-Yeany for a speech contest about "Freedom" in my Civics class.

I wondered if Do-Yeany was happier in the United States than he was in China. However, language is a barrier between us, and I may never know what he feels.

Vincent, the youngest child in our family, crawled around the living room of my father's flat. He begged "Goompa," as he affectionately called his great-grandfather, to play squad cars with him. I will always remember the sparkle in Dad's eyes as he watched Vincent play with his toys. To my great relief after the initial phone conversation, Dad seemed happy.

No Chinese reunion would be complete without a feast. That night we met at one of the family restaurants in Chinatown for a banquet, and what a feast it was! I loved everything except the jellyfish tentacles, sea cucumber and tripe. I can still taste the earthy roasted squab, hear the crunch that gave way to the succulent flesh of the whole, crispy fish, and the taste on my fingertips after cracking my favorite crabs with ginger and green onions.

As if that was not enough, the following morning, we feasted on my favorite Chinese food, dim sum. Dim sum means "small meals to delight your heart."

In the restaurants in Chinatown, carts, carrying an assortment of small dishes (cha siu bao, ha gow, siu mai, bok tong go), wove around the tables. I savored every morsel and asked Dad to teach me how to pronounce the Chinese names of my favorite dishes. I wrote the words down in phonetics, so that I would remember how to pronounce them.

I wanted to be able to order dim sum for myself after Dad was gone. Afterwards, we walked through Chinatown, as was our tradition whenever we visited Dad. I will never forget the bright colors, the sounds, and the smells—even the strong and stinky ones—of my hometown.

I knew I had fulfilled my filial duty, but I also knew Dad would never admit what he did or ask forgiveness.

He will never say, "I am sorry." He got away with everything. I must let it go.

Less than a year after the reunion, Dad's health deteriorated. He died on May 8, 1990.

CAROLE LOUIE

Chapter 4

SKELETONS IN THE CLOSET

May 1990
Sunnyvale, California

Florence met Mark and me at San Jose Airport. As we sat at Florence's dining table, she updated us on the details of Dad's illness, about his final days, and about the funeral arrangements, but I had a tough time concentrating on what she said. I was so angry that Dad died without saying he was sorry for what he did to our family—what he did to me—I felt as if hands choked my neck.

I needed to tell my brother and sister my secret. "I want to. I need to..." I said. Taking a deep breath in, I continued, "I need to tell you something." They both turned to me at the same time. Mark sat stoically, but Florence touched my hand and said, "It's okay. We're here."

"I cannot keep this inside any longer. You know I always felt that it was my fault Mom and Dad had to get married. Imagine Mom going back home to Florida and trying to explain giving birth to a Chinese baby to her Southern family. The irony is that I do not look Chinese." I said. "And then, when we finally did run away, it must have been hell for her every time she looked at me, a constant reminder of the reason she had to marry a Chinese man. But there's something else."

Florence held my hand in hers. Her hand felt like an anchor keeping my mind from drifting aimlessly.

"Before we left Dad in 1957, something happened." I turned to Mark, "Do you remember when you and I traded beds? I slept with Dad when you had to sleep on the cot in Mom's room. Sometimes, you had a tent over you because you had a breathing problem. Do you remember when suddenly I slept with Florence and Mom in Mom's bed?"

Mark scratched his chin as if trying to conjure up his memory. Florence raised her eyebrows and leaned forward. I thought I was going to faint. Memories of that night flowed to me.

"One night after we returned from the club, you know, the one where Dad played mahjong, and we watched TV and ate sunflower seeds, Dad had me rub his back with Tiger Balm ointment."

I paused trying to control the bombardment. "Things went downhill from there." My throat tightened, but I knew that I had to continue. I could not keep Dad's secret any longer. "He molested me," I said as if the memories would not hurt if whispered quietly.

"I got away. I ran to Mom's room. I locked the door. Both of you were asleep. I hid on the far side of Mom's bed and watched for his footsteps under the door as I waited for Mom to come home from work that night."

"What did Mom do?" Florence said.

"Mom scolded me for locking the door. When I told her why I locked the door, she said, "Go to sleep now." I crawled in next to you. Mom changed her clothes and got into bed on the other side. She was tired, and she fell asleep quickly. You slept like a baby, but I stayed awake listening for Dad's footsteps outside the bedroom door. I felt relieved when I heard him leave for work the next day. I barely slept for the rest of the time we lived in that house until the day we ran away. So, you see, it was my fault we had to leave." I did not know if they would understand the shame, guilt, and fear I had carried around inside me for years; feelings that coalesced into tears, the first tears since Florence called to tell me Dad was gone.

Mark did not make eye contact. Florence took a deep breath and gave me a hug. "I didn't know. I didn't know," she said.

"It's weird. I must have suppressed what happened, but a few years ago, I began having flashbacks. Every time I saw Dad, I hoped and prayed he'd say, 'I'm sorry.' Now he's gone. I'll never know if he was sorry for what he did or not. What kind of person does that to his child?"

I still did not know what to do with my feelings, so I put a lid on them yet again. I'd have to find a way to heal the wound ripped open again by his death, but at least I told someone else besides my therapist. I let out a breath, laid my head on the table, and wept.

Chapter 5

THE WAKE

May 11, 1990
San Francisco, California

I rang the bell at Dad's and heard footsteps on the stairs. "Calo," Auntie Tai called out in her singsong voice as I climbed the steep stairs.

"Auntie Carole. Auntie Florence," Mabel said, leaning over the rail.

Wai Gauy greeted us, "We will have a meal before we go to the mortuary. Wai Zhen and Shao Yun are in the kitchen finishing the dishes. Vegetarian foods. No meat. Not good before the funeral. Only after."

"Is that a Buddhist custom?" I said since we were not vegetarians, but Wai Gauy did not answer. I headed toward the kitchen to watch my nieces.

The smells from the kitchen transported me back to the time Dad showed me how to prepare food for stir frying. It required a combination of attention and patience, followed by quick actions.

I loved the steady motions of chopping the ingredients and the graceful movements of sliding the ingredients down the side of the wok. Knowing when the meat had marinated to perfection and the oil was hot enough to cook the meat quickly, sealing in the juices, was the secret before adding the rest of the ingredients at the right time.

Watching Shao Yun toss the sauce with the vegetables reminded me of the times I watched Dad cook at the restaurant and at home when I was a little girl. It was the only legacy my father, who was an incredible chef, left me.

We sat at the dining table, but it was difficult for me to eat. Do-Yeany's family did not seem to have the same problem I did. They held the rice bowls to their chins and shoveled the food from their bowls to their mouths quickly. I picked at my food. Jennie picked at her food too. Even though she had attended funerals, I wondered what she would think about experiencing a Buddhist funeral. It was going to be different from the Catholic ceremony for Jennie's Uncle Joe or the Baptist funeral for Grannie.

Speaking quickly in his broken English, Wai Gauy said, "Bow three times at the mortuary to pay our respects. Give offerings and blankets."

I asked about everyone's birth dates, about Dad's brothers and sister and Dad's first trip to San Francisco and made notes in my notepad. Wai Gauy translated for Do-Yeany, "It was in 1928 before the Golden Gate Bridge stood in the bay. His father was an herbal doctor." By bits and pieces, I finally learned something, anything about Dad's family.

I knew that it was common in China for matchmakers to orchestrate arranged marriages, using the Chinese astrological information to determine compatibility as well as how such arrangements would benefit both families. Years later, I learned that marriage connected the "Gold Mountain men," as those who ventured to the United States were called, to their homeland and their filial duties.

"My father was born in 1931, but his mother died soon after," Wai Gauy continued translating in English as Do-Yeany spoke quietly in Chinese. "He was raised by grandfather and grandmother. His father returned to San Francisco before his son's birth." This arrangement may seem strange to Westerners but was part of the Chinese way of life. I wondered how Dad felt about the death of his wife, about leaving his son.

"Auntie Tai," Wai Gauy, hesitated before going on, and I waited patiently. "She's my father's auntie. His mother's sister. She Grandfather's true love."

What! She is our aunt. I had no idea.

Do-Yeany continued, and I paid attention. Wai Gauy continued too. "Grandfather died in 1943."

I quickly calculated that my half-brother was only twelve years old. "The Japanese ..." his voice trailed off, unable to finish the sentence. Lost in the long pause and the expression on Do-Yeany's face, I stopped taking notes. My memory of the details is incomplete, but I remember hearing something about Grandmother Louie and other members of the family escaping to Kowloon near Hong Kong and Do-Yeany left behind. Do-Yeany shut down afterward, and I have not been able to piece that part of the story together. Do-Yeany added that Grandmother Louie tried to help Do-Yeany as did our Uncle Don, Dad's younger brother, who also immigrated to the States.

I knew that Dad tried to bring Do-Yeany to America after the death of Mao Zedong. Finally, in 1978 at the age of forty-seven, Do-Yeany left his homeland to join his father in San Francisco. It was a huge change in midlife, but he followed the old ways of filial piety even though he did not know this man he called "Father."

I pieced together what I could of our family tree, but wanting to know more, appointed myself "family historian" and carried paper and pen with me for the next two days hoping to catch more information about our family saga.

Before we left Dad's house, Wai Gauy gave us symbols of our relationship in the clan. Yam Oy, Florence and I wore small white ribbons in our hair.

The grandchildren and great-grandchildren wore green ribbons in their hair. The men wore black ribbons on their jacket pockets. Wai Gauy said, "The coffin will be open. When we go into the mortuary, everyone should go up to the coffin and bow three times. Stella will guide us through the rest."

Stella, our Chinese liaison, greeted us at Green Street Mortuary. She adorned us with more symbols: black armbands on the right arm and black veils for the daughters, black armbands on the right arm and a black band around the waist for the sons, black armbands for the grandchildren and great-grandchildren and one for Auntie Tai.

The door to the sanctuary opened. Peaceful music soothed my soul as we entered. As the eldest son, Do-Yeany entered first and proceeded to the half-opened coffin. Mark, the second son, followed. I was next, followed by Florence and Yam Oy. The rest of the family followed us, one-by-one, in order of rank.

I held my breath as I stepped closer and closer. I took deep breaths when it was my turn to bow three times and view the body of my father. The illness had taken a toll on him since I had seen him last June. Dad's face looked drawn as if he had lost a lot of weight. He looked like the figures we saw in the Ripley's Wax Museum on Fisherman's Wharf.

His fedora was propped next to his head, and he wore a boutonniere on the lapel of a suit jacket that Auntie Tai made for him.

"That not me. I here. Why you not see me?" Dad's ghost said as he followed me to the first pew on the left. I did not hear him, but I felt cold as if the temperature suddenly dropped ten degrees.

Stella motioned Do-Yeany to join her at the casket and gave him a bowl of water. He sprinkled the water on Dad's face to purify him for the other side. Stella placed a jade ring on Dad's right hand, a watch on his left wrist and a coin between his lips; symbolically, the coin was surrendered to spirits demanding money as the deceased traveled to the spirit world.

Floral arrangements surrounded the coffin, but three stood out to me. One to the left of the casket with red and white flowers forming a large outer circle, with pink flowers surrounding a clock set at 5:00, Dad's time of death, in the inner circle. Banners hung at the bottom on the arrangement with names in both Chinese calligraphy and English. Another large, rectangular arrangement of white carnations surrounded a photograph of Dad. A small spray of white orchids in the lower left corner counter-balanced a larger one of red anthuriums on the upper right corner where a dove perched holding a stream of ribbon in its mouth.

The third arrangement, which stood next to the alcove to the right of the coffin, was a sort of a quatrefoil shape, and elaborately covered with pink and white flowers surrounding a bouquet of orchids. The border was a pleated orchid-colored ribbon, and it also had banners hanging down at the bottom with more writing in calligraphy.

In an alcove, a small tea table held a pig's head, a chicken, three cups of tea (one cup for heaven, one cup for the earth, and one cup for a man), and a dish of the meal we had eaten before the service. Stella knelt on the rug and pointed to the hammered brass urn filled with Joss sticks (incense). We approached the makeshift altar in the same order in which we had filed into the room, accepted the Joss sticks, bowed three times, and placed the sticks into the urn. Such a familiar feeling: wood pushing into the sand, the fragrance of sandalwood filling me with memories, speaking to ancestors long gone. Next, Stella handed us papers containing greetings to go to the netherworld as the messages burned in the free-standing fireplace. Shao Yun and Wai Zhen, dutiful daughters-in-law, helped George and Mabel with this part of the ritual to honor their ancestor.

I had no idea what all this meant, but I went through the rituals like a mouse through a maze. I felt frustration more than grief. My frustration turned into curiosity when the little old woman who sat next to Auntie Tai on the right side of the sanctuary got up and walked toward the coffin.

Even though it was May, she was bundled up in a gray plaid jacket and wore a black knit cap with a black and white band. Wai Gauy informed me that she came to the United States on the same boat with Dad, and she was his spiritual sister. A petite, small boned woman who commanded my attention as she gracefully swayed a tissue thin, pale yellow paper decorated with red writing and Chinese zodiac charts over Dad's body. She rocked to the left and the right, and back again, chanting softly. Then, she folded the paper and gently placed it over his hands. She moved slowly, as if she floated, back to the pew next to Auntie Tai. She seemed mysterious and familiar at the same time.

The Director opened the casket lid completely exposing the lower half of Dad's body and a pile of blankets, "family blankets." Do-Yeany and Yam Oy lead the family in the ceremony of covering Dad's legs with blankets. Mark followed, then Florence and I added our blankets and bowed. Each member of the family including the children added a piece of cloth and bowed.

The private family proceedings completed, and visitors made their way to pay their respects.

Dad's ghost stood by the coffin. He touched the blankets, read the banners on the floral arrangements, surveyed the food offerings on the table, and the ashes of the paper greetings in the fireplace.

"My life wasted. What I thought make me happy, not so good. Now, what do? If only you hear me, Calo. Hear me," he pleaded as he watched me walk back up the center aisle.

I took a few last pictures, thankful that the camera allowed me to take zoom shots, but even this far away, I felt a shiver course through my body. I bowed and said, "Goodbye, Daddy."

"Why can't you hear me, Calo? I here." Dad's ghost followed me as I joined the rest of the family.

As we left, everyone received a piece of candy to help us remember the sweet times. We returned to Dad's house, where Do-Yeany's family dipped their fingers in the dish of water with leaves placed on the dining table after the meal we had eaten before the wake.

Wai Gauy said, "Wash your face to wash away sorrow." We followed suit. He took a piece of candy from the second dish on the table and put it in his mouth. He said, "Remember sweet times."

Shao Yun and Wai Zhen served a meal which consisted of meat. Again, Do-Yeany's family shoveled the food in the rice bowl held to their chins while I picked at my food.

The drive back to Florence's house was quiet, so I reviewed my notes and looked for loose ends that I should tie up the next day.

I was even more curious about the meanings of the rituals. I looked at the death certificate. It stated that Dad was a widow. Even if you did not count Auntie Tai because they did not marry, why wasn't Dad's status listed as divorced instead of widowed? Something, maybe a lot of things, did not feel right, and I wrestled with how I would discover what was true and what was not.

Chapter 6

THE FUNERAL

May 12, 1990
San Francisco, California

The next day, Florence, Jennie, Laura, and I dressed in white, but my brother's family dressed in black.

"Why does Do-Yeany's family not wear white? Have mourning customs changed that much in China?" I said to Florence. I had studied Feng Shui and knew that the color of mourning in the Chinese tradition was white because it represents purity. I did not want to wear the white cotton, cone-shaped hats like the older days, but I felt that it was appropriate to wear white to honor our ancestor.

"Maybe, it has something to do with being raised under the Communist regime. Who knows?" Florence said.

We gathered at the mortuary and donned veils, and armbands. We lined up in silence as if on autopilot into the order we learned the day before and filed into the sanctuary, bowed to our ancestor.

We assumed our rightful places on the pews. I noticed right away that something was missing. What had happened to the food?

I was surprised when Father Timothy Tam from the United Methodist Church took over the service. Did Dad arrange this part of the service for us, his Amer-Asian offspring, or did he do it to ensure his status with the Christian God? Dad told me that he'd denounced the Christian God when his first wife died. He had prayed to Him for her safety when she gave birth, but he felt that God did not answer his prayers, so how good could He be? I understood Dad wanting to cover all the bases.

Auntie Tai was visibly upset during this part of the ceremony. She muttered under her hand, making it difficult to hear what Father Tam said. That was her intention.

Dad's ghost stood next to her and watched as she looked down at her hand and the jade band she wore. He felt responsible for her sorrow. They'd never married but wore the bands as if they were.

He'd made sure he had provided for her after he died, and yet, now he sensed that she not only felt alone but also scorned sitting on the opposite side instead of with the family. He looked up at Father Tam. He saw that this man's presence upset her. He had thought she'd accept what he did for his funeral just as she had for everything he did in life.

Dad should have known. She was a faithful Buddhist, always starting the day before the family altar.

"Aiya! I will never be at peace. I should have..." He couldn't finish. He couldn't say the words aloud.

Father Tam did a beautiful job delivering the eulogy in Chinese and then, in English. I do not remember what he said but, one word replayed in my mind: afterlife. I did not completely resonate with Christian beliefs about heaven and hell, and I was curious about Buddhism and Taoism.

Father Tam's service was short, to the point, and then, it was time for a final farewell. The director opened the casket for the last time.

As I approached the coffin, conflicting emotions flooded every part of my body. *Why did you hurt me, hurt our family? We've lost our chance to heal the past. Damn it!* Surprised by the rush of anger, I could not hold back my tears, the only way I knew how to express my angry feelings.

I quickly shut down the stream of emotion and stoically walked in step with the rest of the family as we proceeded out of Green Street Mortuary and got into the cars waiting to take us to the cemetery.

In days gone by, a proper Chinese family would have spent a lot of money on mourners and the procession. Hired mourners would wail and lament the loss of the deceased. Often musicians helped with cacophonous noises of cymbals, drums, and horns that warded off evil spirits. Family members usually fell in line in stoic fashion.

Modern times modified this ancient tradition. There were no professional mourners. There was less ceremony than before, but we joined in the procession as the Green Street band led the way.

The mortuary attendants placed the casket into the black hearse, the second car. My nephews, Wai Gauy and Wai Kim, held up the floral arrangement with the large photograph of Dad in the backseat of the first car, a black Cadillac convertible. Do-Yeany placed a long joss stick into an incense holder at the front of the Cadillac and took his place in the third vehicle with Yam Oy, Auntie Tai, Shao Yun, Wai Zhen, and the children. I joined the Amer-Asian family in the next car.

Although I have seen a procession from the street many times, it was different being on the inside gazing at the onlookers.

Some folks on the street were Chinatown tourists who did not understand the rituals' others were the older Chinese who gathered to watch reverently as another old one, who may have been a distant relative or friend, proceeded to the last part of his sojourn.

The Green Street Mortuary Band played "Onward Christian Soldiers" as the procession headed up Stockton, past Jackson Street where Mark and I were born and where Dad died in the Chinese Hospital. Because Dad did not live in Chinatown, as the procession made its way left on Clay Street, we paused at the entrance of the Soo Yuen Association. Slowly, solemnly, the band marched, and we followed, left onto Grant Avenue where the cavalcade passed by Cousin Pak's restaurant, Louie's on Grant Avenue. Finally, the band pulled over to the sidewalk, and we passed by Chinatown and headed to Colma. The melody "Amazing Grace" grew faint as we headed to Woodlawn cemetery south of San Francisco.

The service at the gravesite was brief. The mortuary attendant took the photo of Dad out of the floral arrangement and gave it to Do-Yeany. The attendants lowered the casket. One by one, each person discarded his band or veil.

Holding my veil, black band, and white ribbon in my hand, I looked down at the pieces of fabric that dotted the copper top of Dad's casket as the sun peaked out from the passing cloud and bounced off the copper top blinding me. Something moved to my right and goose bumps covered my body.

"I know you're here. I just know it," I said, "but how can I talk with you. Is it too late?"

"Calo, I know you see me. Can you hear me? Aiya! What I done? If had one more hour."

I threw the pieces of fabric onto the coffin in the bottom of the hole in the earth. "Goodbye, Daddy," I said one last time.

Dad's ghost followed us to the banquet at one of the family restaurants back in Chinatown. He wanted a drink of Mao Tai, a clear alcoholic drink served straight up, and a taste of his favorite foods but he knew he had to wait for the food left at the Festival of the Hungry Ghost.

After the banquet, Cousin Jek and his wife, Fay, escorted Mark, Florence, Bob, Laura, Jennie, and me to the Soo Yuen Association Center on Clay Street. Dad's ghost watched as we went one way and Do-Yeany's family went the other way.

"No! No! You go together. Go together. Not..." Dad's voice trailed off into the streets of San Francisco, but no one heard him.

Something is not right, and I want to know the truth.

James On Louie 1940s

James On Louie (1980s)

Do-Young, Yam Oy, Wai Kim, and Way Gauy Louie
in China (1950s)

Meeting Do-Young (1979)

Reunion (1989)

Photos from the funeral services

Tombstone for James On Louie and Tai Hung Lee

Soo Yuen Association

Tombstone for Hung Don Louie

Grandmother Louie (Lee Yuet Ping), Louie Hung Him, Louie Hung Hor, Louie Hung Hay, Louie Hop Yee (daughter), and Louie Do-Young (China 1930s)

Grandmother Louie with family and friends (Kowloon 1958)

Louie Do-Young and Yam Oy

Louie Do-Young, Yam Oy, Wai Kim, and Wai Gauy

Louie Hung On (photo on left from 1927 before his first trip to U.S., photo on the right from 1929 upon return trip to China)

James "Jimmy" On Louie (his American name) 1959

Louie Mow 1907

Louie Mow aka Louie Hong Wei 1910

Louie Mow aka Louie Hong Wei 1927

Louie Fat aka Louie Tin Hock 1881

Louie Fat aka Louie Tin Hock 1907

Louie Fat aka Louie Tin Hock 1916

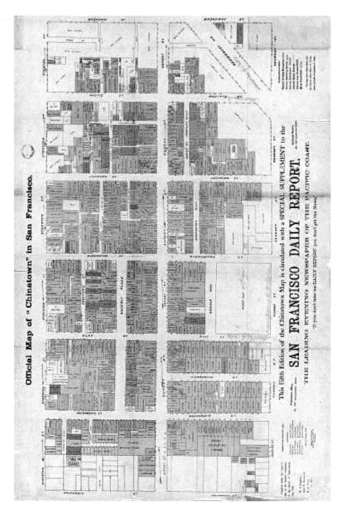

San Francisco Map 1880s

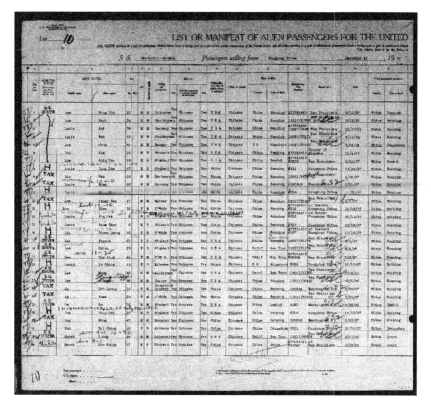

Passenger Manifest December 1927 with
Louie Hung On (line 11)

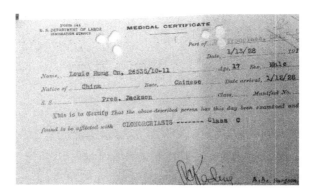

Medical Certificate for Louie Hung On 1928

26535/10-11   2-8-28 - Pg. 14.

Q When, where and to whom were you married? A CR-16-10-8 (November 1, 1927) in GONG YICK CITY, to LEE SHEE.
Q How long were you home after you were married? A Not quite a month.

(PERSONAL DESCRIPTION: Height: 5'2" in American shoes; pit over outer corner of right eyebrow; large scar right neck; pin mole in left ear; numerous small line scars all over face; black hair; brown eyes; medium complexion.)

Q What are your father's name, age and present whereabouts? A LOUIE MOW and LOUIE HONG WEE, 39 years old, now a merchant in the WAH SANG LUNG CO., 667 Grant Avenue, San Francisco.
Q When did you last see your father in China? A I saw him before he left home in CR-15-3 (April 1926). He arrived home in CR-14-7 (August 1925).
Q Did you ever see him before that in China? A Yes, when he was in China from CR-10 to CR-13 (1921 to 1924).
Q Do you remember him prior to that at home in China? A No.
Q What are your mother's name, age and place of birth? A LEE SHEE, 36 years old, has natural feet, now living in GONG YICK CITY.
Q How many times has your father been married? A Once only.
Q What is your intention in coming to this country? A To study English and to learn business.
Q Do you intend to live with your father? A Yes.

APPLICANT FURTHER STATES:
        I am a Male of the Chinese race; student by occupation; can speak, read and write Chinese only; intend to remain permanently in the U.S.; have never been arrested nor supported by charity; neither I nor either of my parents have ever been an inmate of an insane institution; I have never been deported from this country; I have $5. My father will take care of me.

Q Do you understand what polygamy and anarchy are? A Yes, I understand. I am not a polygamist nor an anarchist nor do I believe in either of them.
Q How many brothers and sisters have you? A Four brothers, one sister.
Q What are their names, ages, and present whereabouts?
A LOUIE HUNG DON, 16 years old, now in GONG YICK CITY.
   LOUIE BOCK ON,   11 years old,   do.
   LOUIE HUNG OR,   7 years old,   do.
   LOUIE HUNG HAY,   5 years old,   do.
   My sister is LOUIE HOCK YEE, 3 years old, living in GONG YICK CITY.
Q Was your father at home when your sister was born? A No.
Q When was she born? A Born CR-15-9-13 (Oct. 19, 1926).
Q Did you ever have any brothers or sisters who died? A No.
Q What are your father's parents' names and whereabouts? A My grandfather, LOUIE FAT, died in CR-8-5-20 (June 17, 1919) in my house in SAM OR VILLAGE. My grandmother is LEE SHEE, now living in GONG YICK CITY.
Q What caused your grandfather's death? A I don't know.
Q Where was he living at the time of his death? A In my uncle's (LOUIE FON) house he died.

One page of hundreds from NARA for Louie Hung On

Wah Sang Lung Co. at 667 Dupont Street/Grant Avenue 1930s

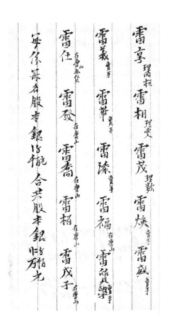

Partner's List for Wah Sang Lung Co.

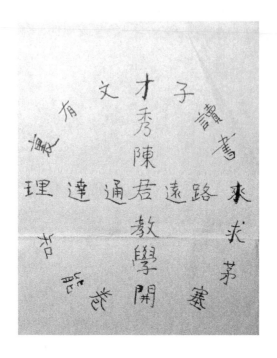

才子讀書來
來求茅塞開
開卷能知理
理裏有文才

才秀陳君教學開
開學教君遠路來
來路遠君通達理
理達通君陳秀才

Louie Hung Don's Poem

Carole with cultural exchange group from the
American Society of Interior Design 1985

Carole with Friends of Roots Group 2016

San Duo/Sam Dor Village – Baidu Maps

San Duo elder – lady with the pink chair

Hong May/Keng Wei Village – Google Maps

Hong May/Keng Wei Village

Carole meditating on property of
Louie Fat/Louie Tin Hock

Carole honoring her ancestors

Carole with Friends of Roots Group
and Lei Rongyang, village chief

Carole found a photo of Louie's of Grant Avenue
(San Francisco, CA) at the Guangdong Overseas
Chinese Museum

Louie's of Grant Avenue – San Francisco, CA

Chapter 7

Soo Yuen Association

1990
San Francisco, California

I whispered to Florence as we crowded in the elevator, "Can you believe we're going to the Soo Yuen Association at last?"

In 1977, I found journals from the association at Dad's apartment. I read the articles and stories written in English hoping to learn more about my Chinese heritage. I thought the association was the place Dad played Mahjong and the center for the Chinese Diaspora, but I found something more as I studied the picture of the founders and the wall hanging that graced the walls of the center.

Cousin Jek said, "This photograph of the founders." Men in dark skirts and robes with shaved foreheads.

So, that's what they looked like one hundred years ago!

"In 1881, several men organized the Soo Yuen Association to help Chinese sojourners from the Louie, Fong, and Kwong families make their way on Gam Saan, the Gold Mountain. They left their families to try to find gold, to become wealthy and to help their families in China." Pointing to the photo of the founders, he said, "These men met the ships that came in, called out their family names in their dialect, and welcomed the travelers to the new world."

Many sojourners found a life of servitude and other injustices. The ones who were clever began to understand the ways of the Americans and started organizations all over Chinatown to help their fellow compatriots.

I imagined the comfort of knowing they would not be alone in this strange place. I looked at the picture of the founders in their long robes and queues, long braids that showed their loyalty to the emperor. Cutting their hair meant the death penalty. I visualized them walking up and down the hills of San Francisco. I imagined them being so far away from their families, adjusting to a new world, and looked down upon by the white Americans. I envisioned an air of dignity about them as they banded together in their secret enclaves to outwit their adversaries.

"See this wall hanging? It tells the story about the Louie, Fong, and Kwong people," Cousin Jek continued like a docent in a museum, "We have a common ancestry that dated back to the time of the Yellow Emperor, Huang Ti, 2697-2598 B.C."

Until that moment, I thought Huang Ti was a mythical figure, but per the wall hanging, our ancestor, Louie Jo, was the emperor's wife and the one responsible for the cultivation of silk from the silkworm's cocoon.

It surprised me when Cousin Jek said, "That your daddy's signature," tapping on the glass to the name of the translator at the bottom of the hanging.

I turned away to hide my feelings.

"Are you okay?" Florence said.

"I had asked Dad to bring me here so many times, and now I am finally here. Why did it take his death to make it happen?" My tears came from so many missed opportunities, but also, they were tears of joy to know more about my heritage.

CAROLE LOUIE

Chapter 8

A RELUCTANT MEDIUM

1992
Naples, Florida

Dad's ghost finally understood what he did not when he walked the earth: that I was sincere in wanting to know about our ancestors and his life in China and the U.S. We both discovered that it was not too late. He began to tell me his story.

"You call Stera. She help you," Dad said the next morning after he came to me in my meditation class. And then, as if to make sure I understood the urgency of his request, he pushed my shoulder. "Call Stera. She 'splain you Buddha Hell. Do now."

I looked at my watch and calculated the time difference between Naples, FL, and San Francisco, CA. Okay, I guess there is no time like now. *What will Stella say when I tell her why I want to know what the Tenth Hell of the Buddha is? I think I'll just be honest with her about Dad coming to me.*

To my delight, Stella was very helpful. She not only explained what the Tenth Hell is all about but also told me that she worried about the Feng Shui/Geomancy of Dad's gravesite. I'd studied Feng Shui for many years, so I understood what Stella meant when she told me that the direction of the head of Dad's gravesite was incorrect. She feared for Dad's spirit. Feng Shui/Geomancy determined the burial sites of the emperors because an auspicious location affected the wellbeing of the deceased's descendants. "He'll be a hungry ghost." I heard the fear in her voice.

"A what?"

"Hungry Ghost. Wander the earth when not in hell. He cannot go to heaven unless,"

"Unless what?" I asked.

"Buddhist monks can do the ceremony."

I could tell this was going to be expensive, and Dad must have had the same thought because he whispered in my ear, "You do it. You understand. Save money. Tell Stera, 'Thank you,' then you will do it."

"Okay, Stella. I understand, but Dad is telling me to do whatever needs to be done. Can you just explain the ritual to me?" *Another ritual. Great! I hate ceremonies, but this is for my dad, so what can I do?*

I did the ceremony just as Stella directed. I burned the incense as well as a makeshift paper petition to speak to the Buddha of the Tenth Hell. I made an offering on the altar, which I created on my coffee table. As the incense curled its smoke trails in the air, I felt unsure if this ritual was going to work since I was not a Buddhist monk or even Buddhist for that matter. I didn't know the Buddhist chants, so I put on the Buddhist chanting music. I said, "Lord Buddha, I forgive Dad for what he did. Please free his spirit to go on to his next life." The one thing Stella forgot to tell me was to do the ritual outside. I did not discover until many years later that I should have made the offerings to hungry ghosts outside of one's home so that the spirit would not be invited into or stay in the home. Honestly, I don't think it would have made any difference because once Dad started talking, he was like the little child who tugged at his mommy's dress until noticed, and once noticed, wouldn't stop talking. That's how the conversations with my father's ghost began.

Next, Dad urged me to translate the words carved in calligraphy on his tombstone.

I met my translator Li Jie in 1985 when I traveled to China. He was one of my national tour guides. We connected as if we had always known one another.

When I was in China, I discovered that most Chinese did not understand my name, Louie, until I showed them the calligraphy for the word. Then they'd reply, "Oh, yes, yes, yes. Thunder. Lei, in Mandarin."

Li Jie spoke in the Mandarin dialect, which was influenced by the Mandarins, the learned public officials. My father, born in 1910 in Taishan, China during the reign of the last emperor, Puyi, spoke in the Taishanese dialect. Since Dad's birth and the Communist take-over, putanghua became the national language and the old Wade-Giles Romanization system of transliteration converted to pinyin, the official phonetic system used after the Chinese revolution to translate the Chinese language into a Romanized form of spelling. I doubt that my father knew the Wade-Giles system. Like many Taishanese, he seemed to make up his system of transliteration, but the calligraphy was the same regardless of the dialect.

When Li Jie translated Dad's tombstone, I discovered that Dad was from San Duo village, Tang Mian Town, Taishan, China. I had the name, but I still did not have the actual location until 2002 when I located Taishan, China on the Internet. I discovered that Taishan had a population of about one million, but it would take many more years before I found San Duo village.

***

Dad's ghost sheepishly hinted at terrible things in the past, but I persisted following the crumbs of information he whispered to me until I unraveled the story of the early Chinese immigrants, who were predominantly from Taishan. It was not a pretty story.

The United States abolished slavery by the time of the wave of Chinese immigration in the mid-1800s, but many people considered the Chinese people inferior even though they worked hard in the gold mines and on the Transcontinental Railroad. Until October 1948, it was illegal for a Caucasian to marry a person of color, including an Asian, in California. I was born in October 1947.

I had suspected that I was the result of an unwanted pregnancy between a white woman and a yellow man, and possibly, conceived out of wedlock. That's no big deal these days, but in 1947, it was taboo. Two plus two seemed to add up to three in my case. It should not have mattered, but it was like a burr under my saddle.

When I found Lisa See's book, *On Gold Mountain*, I felt as if I'd found a friend, someone who understood my Chinese American or Amer-Asian experience. Although I am not as fair-skinned as my mother or Lisa See, I do not look Chinese, and yet, like Lisa See, I feel Chinese.

During Dad's next visit, he said, "Get out birth certificate."

"Okay," I said wondering what rabbit hole this train of thought was going to take me down. I looked at the paper, and for the first time, I saw something I had never noticed before. It was as if it glowed in neon lights. The document listed my mother's race as Chinese.

"What! Chinese! Mom no more looks Chinese than..." I couldn't finish the sentence because I suddenly remembered Adeline Yen Mah's book, *Falling Leaves. The Memoir of an Unwanted Chinese Daughter*, and her stepmother, who was Eurasian and who could pass for a relative of my mother. I was sure Dad made this error intentionally to protect us from the miscegenation laws.

"Now, you understand why I say, 'Be American.' Safer that way," he said.

"Yes, I am beginning to understand. The Gold Mountain was not what you expected it to be, was it?"

Chapter 9

MAKING AMENDS

1996
Naples, Florida

As I learned to accept my gifts as a medium, Dad learned with me. I cannot begin to explain how this works, by osmosis between this world and the next. I believe he observed me as much as I observed him, especially when I wrote my thoughts in my journal, or read a book about reincarnation, or meditated to music.

Our next lesson was about the cause and effect of our actions. It is known as the Law of Karma in Buddhism or "what you sow is what you reap" in Christianity; in other words, *what goes around comes around.*

"Calo. It's Ching Ming time and I do not do Ching Ming for Don. You do for me," Dad said one morning in March.

"I'm not sure what you're talking about," I said.

"Ching Ming. Honor ancestor day." He tapped the book on my desk.

I flipped through the book I'd just received, *Mooncakes and Hungry Ghosts: Festivals of China* (Carol Stephanchuk and Charles Wong), to the chapter about the Festivals of the Dead. There it was: "Clear Brightness Festival (April 4, 5, or 6) Qingming Jie: an annual ritual to honor one's ancestors by going to their gravesites, maintaining the surroundings, and giving offerings of food, effigies, and incense."

"But I don't even know where Uncle Don is buried," I said, "You did not tell me when he died, so I could not attend his funeral."

"I need pay respects to Don," he said, but what he meant was that I needed to pay respects to my uncle for him. Dad and Uncle Don walked a fine line between old traditions and new ones. Dad was conveniently modern when it suited him, such as when he got together with my mother, but he clung to old Chinese traditions when it came to lording over his brother. Dad was the patriarch of the family. I do not know the details of why Dad and Uncle Don had a falling out after we ran away from Dad in 1957, but it was so intense that even after Mark, Florence, and I reunited with Dad, he did not allow Uncle Don near us.

I'll never forget the time I saw Dad in 1969. Just as I was leaving, I saw the silhouette of Uncle Don walking toward us, but Dad told us to leave before Uncle Don arrived.

Dad did the same thing when Mark and Florence visited. It was a loss we will never forget. However, on a visit with Dad in 1978, Dad took me to see my dying uncle at a nursing home. Uncle Don was not able to talk, but his eyes lit up when I talked about his photography invention and his beautiful photographs. I said, "You are always my favorite uncle."

Finally, Dad was ready to let go of his grudge—his need to be the authority figure. He was ready to ask for forgiveness and to honor his brother as an equal.

Then, I received a call from a private investigator who was searching for the descendants of James On Louie, the brother of Don Louie. The investigator found money in a bank account and needed to verify the descendants who were eligible to receive the monies. The process opened the dialog between Wai Gauy, Do-Yeany's son/spokesperson, and me. He told me that Dad buried Uncle Don in the old Chinese cemetery, but he did not tell me the location of the cemetery or Uncle Don's gravesite.

When Dad knew he was dying, he chose Woodlawn Cemetery because he liked the grounds better than the old Chinese cemetery. We would soon find out why.

I decided to go to California with the hopes that I would find Uncle Don's gravesite. Florence and I drove to the well-manicured grounds of Woodlawn to pay our respects at Dad's gravesite.

We asked the person at the office for directions to the Chinese Cemetery. He laughed as he explained there was no attendant at the Chinese cemetery to direct us to the exact location, but he gave us the address and told us how to get there. He said, "The cemetery is on a steep hill and it will be next to impossible to locate your uncle's gravesite."

Florence and I decided to try. The Chinese Cemetery, Hoy Sun Ning Yung Cemetery, was ominous compared to Woodlawn. The hill was steeper just as the folks at Woodlawn had warned us. I looked around the hillside, hoping and praying that we were safe, not from ghosts but from anyone who might prey on mourners. I wondered if we would find Uncle Don's grave. Chinese calligraphy inscribed on the tombstone and a photograph identified of the deceased. I could read the calligraphy character for "Louie," but I had no idea how to read Uncle Don's Chinese name.

"Thank goodness Chinese people put the picture of the deceased on the tombstone. I hope Dad included Uncle Don's photo," I said to Florence as she headed in one direction and I veered toward the right. We agreed to talk to Dad and Uncle Don to ask their help with our search. I began to walk, intuitively following an urge to go to the right. Florence headed up the hill to the next level. It did not take long. I recognized the picture of my uncle's rounded face immediately and called out to Florence, "Over here. I can't believe it. I found it."

"Wow! That was quick. Dad and Uncle Don must not want us to stay here too long. This place gives me the creeps."

Florence and I cleaned the gravesite, burned incense, joss papers, and I said a prayer. Dad and Uncle Don watched as we performed the rituals dutifully. Afterward, they walked away arms wrapped around one another, and disappeared into the foggy mist. Florence wrapped her arms around me, and we vowed that we would never hold a grudge with one another.

Chapter 10

A SPIRT WEDDING

2006
Richmond, Virginia

Dad became so agitated that he began moving the vertical blinds to get my attention. I eventually figured out Dad was upset because Auntie Tai had died, and the family did not do the proper rituals. In fact, Wai Gauy did not tell me that Auntie Tai died in 2004.

Dad became insistent that I perform a spirit wedding for him and Auntie Tai. "Look up," he said, "Hungry Ghost book."

I knew the book he meant, so I consulted *Mooncakes and Hungry Ghosts: Festivals of China.* "There it is. Why didn't I see that before?"

Per the book, "Spirit unions occurred because a young girl who died in childhood decides some years later that she needs a husband to give her children. Her 'children,' who are the living man's offspring from a real marriage, are then obliged to worship the ghost as their mother, providing it with offerings as though she had married when alive."

Dad believed a spirit wedding would make up for not making his union with Auntie Tai legally binding before he died; therefore, obligating his children to honor Auntie Tai as an ancestor.

Dad's first marriage was an arranged one. In fact, most marriages in all cultures were arranged marriages of some sort until recently. Like other cultures, the traditional Chinese marriage was a union formed to assure the continuation of the family lineage. Chinese families are patrilineal, which means that descent is through the men. They are also patriarchal with the hierarchy organized from the senior male downward. Females were not valued in the same way as males, in part, because women left their birth families when they married. Daughters were considered "guests" in the birth family's home. In the old days, females not only became part of the husband's family and household, some never saw their birth families again. Others only visited their birth families at certain times of the year.

It was common for several generations to live together either under the same roof or within a compound. That was the way of life for thousands of years in China and it would have been that way for my dad had he not been one of those who traveled to the United States in the early 1900s.

Families consulted matchmakers to find suitable mates for marriageable sons. The marriage of the number one son was of utmost importance. Marriage was even more important for a son who went abroad. The intention was to ensure his attachment to his family and homeland. The family looked for a bride with a good family status both for her beauty and physical attributes to bear children, as well as her compatibility to her mate as determined by the Chinese horoscope, which was also used to determine the most auspicious date for the wedding ceremony.

I can only imagine Dad's first marriage to Lee Yook Moi/Yook Moi Lee or the anticipation that swept through the household when she became pregnant. However, the joy did not last because she died a few days after Do-Yeany's birth. The year was 1931. My grandparents raised Dad's first son because he had returned to San Francisco. Some sons made their fortunes and returned home as heroes. Others who went overseas were away for many years, even decades. Others never returned.

By the 1940's, Dad worked as a chef in a restaurant on Market Street which is where he met my mother who worked as a waitress. Mom was twenty-two years old; Dad was thirty-five. Mom had run away from the farm in the Florida Panhandle and ended up in San Francisco by way of New Orleans and Miami.

California did not repeal the miscegenation law, which forbade marriage between Caucasians and Asians, until October 1948. When I asked Mom about the miscegenation laws, she said that Dad drove her out-of-state where a justice-of-the-peace married them. I was shocked when I learned this but did not ask which state much less the date. Mom did not volunteer the information, but her silence told me I had stirred up old memories she would rather forget.

My memories of their marriage are more horrific than happy. Mom ran away from Dad twice, once when I was two-years old and the second time when I was nine. I cannot blame her for running away rather than staying in an abusive relationship. She did what she had to do to survive. I felt sorry for Mom, but in a way, I felt sorry for Dad, too, and the image of him returning home from work to find an empty house. At the same time, I felt angry with Dad for creating the situation. Abuse was common in some Chinese families and I wondered if the lack of value placed on women had something to do with this behavior.

Although we did not have much contact with Dad, he wrote to me on occasion. He sent packages with treats from Chinatown. The most memorable letter was the one that told me I had an older brother.

A few years later, another letter told me about Auntie Tai, or at least, that a woman lived with him and I was to call her "Auntie Tai." They lived together for twenty-odd years but did not legally marry. I am not sure why, but I think it had something to do with the money she would lose if they married. I did not know Dad or Auntie Tai well, but I feel that he loved her. It was only after Dad's death that the family told me Auntie Tai, Tai Hung Lee, was the younger sister of Dad's first wife, Yook Moi Lee.

In a traditional Chinese family, Yook Moi Lee would have been the Tai-Tai, the number one wife. My mother would have been the number three wife. Dad was married a second time, but I do not know anything about that marriage. Since Dad and Auntie Tai were not legally married, she would have been a concubine in the ancient tradition.

In a traditional Chinese home, not only did multi-generations live under the same roof, but multiple wives and children also did. Although the patriarch dictated the order, no rule could dictate how a person felt, particularly how one wife felt toward another, how one set of children felt toward another.

I finally understood something Dad had been trying to communicate to me even at his funeral. His biggest regret was not making his union with Auntie Tai binding for our family.

He was furious when he saw her sitting on the "friends" side of the chapel rather than with the family. He said the way to resolve the dilemma was to have a spirit wedding. When the marriage for them was complete, she would be one of our ancestors and honored during the rites of Qing Ming/Ching Ming.

I wrestled with if I should perform these rituals for my father to honor his beliefs even though they are different from my own, how to do the ceremony and whether to include my brothers and sister. Traditionally, the elder son performed the ritual, but I had a feeling that was not an option.

"You do other rituals. You do this one," Dad insisted. So, I made plans to go to California in December 2006 and I knew my first stop had to be the Taoist Temple. I needed to talk to someone who knew about spirit weddings.

I carried the picture of the front door of the temple with me as well as the directions I downloaded from MapQuest. The word "temple" might conjure up an elaborate edifice, but that is not the case for the Tin How Temple at 125 Waverly Place.

The façade of the building is a narrow entrance leading to the Sue Hing Benevolent Association and Tin How Temple. Waverly, a familiar street to the locals is more of an alley, a side street in San Francisco.

As we stood in front of the entrance, I sensed the hundreds of thousands of clansmen who had crossed the threshold in search of help from Mazu, the Chinese sea goddess, even as I sought help for Dad. My sister Florence, and my friend Janet, and I climbed up the flights of stairs.

I did not know what to expect as we climbed the last flight of stairs. I breathed in the familiar smell of incense at the door and saw the haze of smoke created by the incense and burnt offerings. An elaborate altar was to our far left with niches on both sides. Hundreds of banners hung from the ceiling above the altar. Straight ahead of us, more altars flanked a fireplace. To our right, doors opened out to the balcony where, yet two more altars stood: a larger one backed to the balcony railing and a much smaller one was to the right and backed to the exterior wall of the building. The balcony overlooked Waverly Place where the sounds of the streets of Chinatown echoed.

A table to the immediate left of the entrance was set up with paraphernalia needed for rituals. A petite woman, intent on folding papers into shapes that represented lanterns and gold or silver bullion, sat on the chair behind the tables.

She did not speak English but hand-signaled to us that she'd get someone who did. She called out in a singsong voice and Susan appeared. I got right to the point. I introduced my sister, my friend and myself. I hoped she would not think I was crazy when I asked if she knew anything about a spirit wedding.

"Ah, yes. This do for a young girl who die before marrying," she said.

"I know, but this is a slightly different circumstance," I said. I explained that Dad's spirit came to me and told me that he regretted not marrying Auntie Tai before he died in 1990 and now that she had passed over and joined him in the spirit world, he was determined to make things right. She seemed to understand and told us where to purchase the clothes and jewelry needed for Dad and Auntie Tai for the ceremony. We knew where the shop was, and Susan said she would call the woman at the shop and tell her to expect us.

A few minutes later, we perused the stacks of garments. The clothes, shoes, and jewelry for a spirit wedding are paper effigies. I mused at the idea of effigy clothes but another part of me got into the process. Simultaneously, Florence and I knew we found the right clothes for Dad. The herringbone suit, shirt with a combination of stripes and flowers, and geometric patterned tie clashed outrageously – just the way Dad dressed. I nudged Florence, "Does this look like what Dad would wear or what?"

"Perfect," she said, "and here's something Auntie Tai would love." She handed me a package of an orchid and sage colored, floral print suit. Next, we selected shoes and jewelry. The packages included cell phones.

"She'll have to explain cell phones to him," I said imagining them chatting about these details in the spirit world just as we did in the shop. We also purchased a double happiness sign, a wedding lai see (red envelope), and a package that included effigy money. We headed back to the temple, made our way back up the hill to Waverly Place, back up the four flights, and re-entered the temple. The lady, who was still folding papers, called out to Susan.

Our excitement was as palpable as if we were bridesmaids cloistered in the bride's chambers before the wedding. Susan told me to write Dad's name and village on the clothes and Auntie Tai's name on her things, but not to write her ancestral village name because Auntie Tai would become part of Dad's village. I wrote their names on the edge of the stack of money. Susan placed a paper lantern on papers from the first stack, and then placed a stack at each of the altars. Susan carried the clothes to the main altar along with a bowl of candy and tangerines and another with the red wedding envelope filled with effigy money. After she had added incense sticks, we were ready to begin.

Florence and I knelt at the main altar for the goddess Tin How and announced our intention to join Dad and Auntie Tai in marriage. Susan knelt with us and repeated our desires in Chinese.

I did not know it at the time, but Florence told me later that as she knelt there, she asked for a sign. No sooner had she put the thought out there when the smoke from the joss sticks rose, bent in mid-air, and formed a heart shape.

We moved to the altar to the left of the fireplace, the altar of Guan Yu the god of war and Taoist symbol of integrity and loyalty. We announced our intentions to him. We moved to the altar to the right of the fireplace, the altar of Tudi Gong the god of earth, where we invited Dad's and Auntie Tai's spirits into the temple. The smaller altar on the balcony was also for Tudi Gong. We repeated our intentions and Susan guided me back inside to a little room tucked away in the corner to the left. We voiced our desires to the ancestors at the altar with tablets of Tai Shan families that represented the Tai Shan community: me in English, Susan in Chinese.

Finally, we moved to the fireplace where we burned the stacks of papers from the various altars, the effigy clothing, double happiness sign, and the wedding money. Orange flames rose as the heat from the fireplace warmed my face. As I closed my eyes to experience the moment, tinkling bells announced the wedding procession.

My mind's eye saw a tiny red shoe appear out of a red wedding palanquin. Tai Hung Lee appeared in a red wedding dress with a red headdress and beaded veil, the traditional wedding attire.

When she lifted the veil, a young Tai Hung Lee gazed into the eyes of Hung On Louie, who was also in traditional garb, and he, too, appeared young. They broke with tradition by viewing each other at that moment instead of waiting until escorted to the wedding chamber.

"They're wearing traditional red clothes, and they're younger," Florence said.

I said, "You saw it too?"

At that moment, I knew it was more than okay that my sister and I were the ones who performed the ceremony instead of our elder brother because we did it out of love.

Chapter 11

THE CONCUBINE'S DAUGHTER

April 5, 2016
Richmond, Virginia

Although I am not Buddhist, I believe in many of its teachings. Even though I do not care for rituals, I drive to Hue Quang Buddhist Temple to honor my ancestors every year. I park near the twenty-foot tall statue of Guan Yin.

Greeted by the swoosh of lines of flags marking the Ching Ming, the day to honor one's ancestors, I hold the incense sticks to my nose and take in the familiar fragrance, light the incense sticks, and bow three times. I am ready to face the fact that endings are not always happy ever after. I offer my prayer for Dad, for Auntie Tai and all my ancestors but unfinished business still haunts me. Dad has made amends with me, with Uncle Don, his parents, and Auntie Tai. However, he has never mentioned my mother and what he did to her.

"Guan Yin, will Dad and Mom be at peace?" I said to the Goddess of Mercy and Compassion. Her statue towered over the incense burner and me. I felt a being beside me. She exuded calmness that strengthened my resolve. I felt as peaceful as the lotus floating in the pond at Guan Yin's feet. I knew that I must let go.

Neither my mother nor my father was forthcoming about their relationship but the recent revelation that they had not married stirred something inside me. Today, that's no big deal just as interracial marriage is much more accepted. I suspect the conflict between my parents was due as much to their immaturity and human foibles as to their cultural differences. The bottom-line was their relationship was doomed because Dad was abusive, both verbally and physically.

I lived in fear of his temper, especially when he raised his voice. I understood why we ran away from Dad, but I still did not understand the lies—the tangled web of lies that had been both woven and hidden from us for so many years. I believe Mom would have gone to her grave with the lie if it had not been for new rules about driver's license renewal after 9-11 that forced her to reveal the truth. It was challenging to pry the truth from Mom or Dad, but my psyche was persistent and nudged me in ways that defy reason.

When memories from my childhood flashed across the screen of my consciousness, and ordinary psychotherapy did not help me process the memories, I found regression therapy, a form of hypnosis, helpful.

Through regression therapy, I remembered bits and pieces of the first time we ran away from Dad. I did not know it was the first time until I asked my mother about what I saw in my regression and she told me what happened in 1950.

"Not long after Florence was born, and you were about two and a half years old, Daddy had a stroke," Mom said. "I planned to go home to Florida for a visit, but a few days before the trip, Jimmy became angry over some crazy thing—I can't remember what. He hit me and bit me on the neck." She sighed. "I called the police and had him arrested. While he was in jail, I packed the bags and took Mark, Florence, and you to a motel. The next day, I took us to the train station." She paused and shifted the phone from one side to the next and continued her story. "I told you to watch over Mark and Florence while I purchased our tickets."

A vision of that day crept into my memory; I sat in the corner on the hard bench, my sister's stroller, loaded down with baby essentials created a barrier in front of me, and a tattered suitcase completed the barricade on the other side of my brother.

Mom said, "We stayed in Florida almost a year while I helped Mama and Daddy. I looked for work, but I could not find a job and Mama had enough on her hands with Daddy. So, I made the decision to go back to Jimmy."

"Now, it makes sense," I said, "What I saw in my regression was when we returned. I stood at the window as the train neared the station." I remembered more as we talked about the trip back to California: my hands pressed to the glass, I felt anxious and fearful at the same time as I saw my father waiting for us.

I was amazed how my mind hid those memories for fifty years. I was even more astounded by the interweaving of my anticipation and my fear into an emotional knot. I unraveled the cords with my awareness from an adult perspective, an unraveling that helped me sort out my reactions when certain scenes played out in my life such as how I felt when Mom told me to watch over my brother and sister while she purchased the tickets. Even though I was a toddler, an emotional charge flowed through her directive and how I perceived it. I carried that responsibility for too long. Finally, it was time to let it go.

It was also time to let go of my anger toward my parents: toward my father for molesting me, and my mother for not giving me the support I needed afterward. I saw my parents as flawed adults, and yet, I sensed a deeper connection with them, an inexplicable emotional energy.

I accepted my parents just as they were and knew they had done the best they knew how at their level of conscious awareness. I knew that I had been suppressing my feelings about my parents and later, toward other authority figures.

Just as the scene of returning home as a three-year-old had bubbled up in my memory, I felt more images churning on the surface of my conscious awareness like a roiling pot of boiling water. Through spontaneous flashbacks, answers bubbled up into my mind of a connection with my mother and father in another lifetime.

***

A lifetime in China. A young girl. Mei Ling was sold as a concubine to the old wealthy Patriarch to save her family from starvation. I felt her fear and disgust as he entered her bedroom and forced himself on her. How dirty she felt afterward. The Tai-Tai, the number one wife, treated Mei Ling like a slave. Mei Ling felt abused by both and to make matters worse, she felt abandoned by her birth family and yet assumed the responsibility for their survival. Mei Ling felt as helpless and useless as her bound feet. She could not physically run away, but she would find a way to escape.

At first, Mei Ling lost herself in her thoughts until a plan began to take form. She could not walk very far unattended, but she would not stay in this living hell.

The young concubine observed the servants who walked easily on unbound feet, who lifted trays, baskets, and pots with ease. Mei Ling knew she needed to be strong.

She tried picking up a basket filled with clothes, but it seemed impossible. Everyday Mei Ling tried again, and again. She felt the pull in her biceps until one day she could lift the basket a few inches off the floor. She lifted it a little more the next day and the next until she lifted it with an ease she had never known. Of course, she did these exercises unbeknownst to anyone in the household. It wasn't easy, but Mei Ling found ways to sneak away from the family entourage and servants. She wasn't sure why it was important for her to build up her strength, but she felt good that one part of her could feel strong when the rest of her life was so utterly helpless.

Mei Ling lay awake at night while the others slept. The light of the full moon intrigued her. She studied the shadows long after the last person had finally settled within his/her quarters. She listened to the frogs and crickets, the breeze blowing through the bamboo grove. She visualized each part of the garden outside her quarters and even the service garden just beyond the gate. A bustle of noises came from the service garden, especially early in the morning. Servants drew water from the well for Old Cook. They fished a carp out of the pond and gathered fresh vegetables.

Mei Ling became keenly aware of all the sounds in the compound and wondered why she was so oblivious to them before. One morning as the cook prepared a special feast for the Festival of the Hungry Ghost, Mei Ling heard the cook admonish his apprentice, who accidently bumped a pot on the edge of the well. Mei Ling heard the pot hit the walls of the well, but it seemed like a long time before she heard the pot splash as it hit the water. The apprentice tried to catch the pot and almost fell into the well. Luckily, the cook's quick reactions saved the apprentice. "Aiya! It's bad enough I have lost the pot. You could have fallen in, silly useless boy," Old Cook said as he slapped the apprentice on the head.

Mei Ling realized how she would escape.

Festivals were always noisy and busy in the household, so busy that she could get away with all kinds of mischief without being noticed. The next big festival would be the Lunar New Year. In fact, it was their biggest celebration. It was only a few months away, which gave Mei Ling time to put her plan into action.

Each night she listened. By day, she practiced lifting the basket and watching everyone, watching for clues to help her follow through with her plan. She played up to the cook. It wasn't difficult. "How do you make the fish taste so good?" she asked.

He showed her the pond where fresh fish swim among the lemon grass. "The secret is to pluck the fish out moments before it's cooked," he said. In this way, she gained access to the service garden, where Mei Ling looked around and made a mental note of every square inch.

The time for the New Year celebration drew nearer. Mei Ling rehearsed her plan in her mind. On the evening of the Chinese New Year, when everyone was finally asleep, she slipped out of her bed and crawled across the room, keeping her body low. She pulled her body over the threshold, using her upper body strength. From the women's courtyard, she crawled rather than walked, to avoid the risk of falling and waking the family or servants, to the gate that leads to the service courtyard. She deftly moved past the pond and placed a red envelope by a rock where she knew the cook liked to sit. She pressed on towards the well where she used the strength of her arms to pull herself up on the edge of the well.

At last, she would be free, but not before the pain of helplessness broke through the wall she had built around herself. It wasn't as solid as the stone wall of the well. She sobbed for the loss of everything she held dear.

"Damn you, Patriarch. Damn you, Tai-Tai. Damn this hell you've put me in." With those last words, Mei Ling threw her body over the wall, and like the cook's pot, she bounced against the sides of the well and splashed into the dark watery abyss.

The water quickly soaked her quilted robe and pulled her body down. Her body felt heavy, and yet she felt a snap, a jerk, and she knew she was no longer in her body.

Mei Ling's spirit looked down at the lifeless body. She heard noises—Old Cook's padded feet shuffling, the softer step of the apprentice. Old Cook sat at his favorite place on the pond's edge. His hand rested on a red paper envelope, and when he opened it, he found the gold coin. "Merciful heavens!" he exclaimed.

Mei Ling was pleased to see his joy. Then she heard the apprentice scream. He saw her body in the bottom of the well. Cook ran to the apprentice and looked down. "Such a bad omen. Bad luck for the new year." Mei Ling shuddered. She had wanted to punish the Patriarch and Tai-Tai. Now, she realized that others would be hurt. Suddenly, she knew her attempt to be free was in vain.

An old woman appeared. She motioned to Mei Ling to follow her. "Amàh, what have I done?" Mei Ling's Amah wrapped her arms around Mei Ling and silently guided her through the gateway to the other side.

***

Mei Ling's curse on the Patriarch and Tai-Tai created a powerful emotional charge between my parents and me. We came together again as an opportunity to heal the past.

I saw my parents not only as imperfect adults but also as unconscious beings acting from a script played out hundreds of years ago, in another life. There was something very potent in this memory. Not only did the memories give me a deeper understanding of my present life but it helped me "connect the dots" about many issues that ordinary psychotherapy could not help me work through.

I wanted to know more about reincarnation. Were the images about Mei Ling memories or merely an archetype? As a Buddhist, my father must have believed in reincarnation. However, we never talked about it when he was alive. Now, it made sense to me why Dad was in the Tenth Hell. If he was the Patriarch in that other life and my father in this one, what would he be in his next life? I wondered how did reincarnation work. As soon as I asked these questions, ghosts suddenly surrounded me. Mei Ling spoke for the group.

"Do you remember us now, Carole?" I looked around. So many different faces, and yet, there was something familiar about them. Young or old, male or female. I recognized something I could not discern. Then, memories of my childhood flashed quickly across my mind—the ghosts that scared me when I was a child.

"I know you. I remember. What do you want with me? I can't believe it. Have you been around all this time?"

"Time is different on this side. We will help you understand. There is so much we want to tell you," Mei Ling said. "Now, you will know your true purpose in this lifetime."

CAROLE LOUIE

Chapter 12

ROOTING FOR TRUTH

2016
Richmond, Virginia

Joining the Roots Plus group in 2016 was like finding a gold vein after exploring through miles in a dark cave. Roots Plus is an off shoot of The Friends of Roots: Him Mark Lai Family History Project. The focus is helping people find their family roots and ancestral villages in Guangdong Province, China which was the starting point for most of the first sojourners.

My conversations with Dad tapered off after the spirit wedding. I sensed that he and Auntie Tai needed private time. I respected that, and I had other demands that drew my attention: my grandson, who was born in 2005, and his sister who followed in 2008.

Occasionally, Dad would watch over me as I experimented with a new recipe. Before he died, one of the few times I was successful in getting him to open was in the kitchen. Although he'd retired from cooking, he delighted in showing me his tricks of the trade about stir frying.

The secret was cutting up all the ingredients before you started and then placing them into the wok in the order of cooking time. So, meats that were dredged with a little bit of corn starch to dry up any excess moisture went first, and then, were set aside. The vegetables that required longer cooking time next and vegetables that cooked quickly last.

"Watch for color of vegetables," he said, "Don't overcook. That secret. Taste fresher that way. No need MSG." He chopped his words the same way he diced food. Ingredients for the sauce go into a bowl. Soy sauce, rice wine, a little sugar, a few red pepper flakes, a dash of sesame oil, stirred together with chopsticks until the sugar dissolved. Lastly, a teaspoon of cornstarch in a small bowl with some water was added. The wok was heated up, then oil was added down the side of the wok, and the sides shimmered with waves of oil that reflected every dimple made from years of use.

"Now, wok ready for meat." He tipped the chopping board, pushed the meat into the wok with his cleaver. The familiar sizzling filled the air like music. "You add these vegetables," he said pointing to the next cutting board filled with carrots, celery and onion slices cut at an angle to increase their cooking surfaces.

"Now, watch." The onion color became semi-translucent. The celery turned a more vibrant green as the carrots glistened bright orange.

He poked a carrot slice with his cooking chopsticks and felt less resistance. "Heat good. Now, add rest." I added the plate that held baby corn, bamboo shoots, and fresh bean sprouts and scallions; tipping the plate, so everything slid into the wok. Again, the sizzle, but this time a popping sound made from the liquid of the vegetables joined the chorus. Then, the sounds subsided, and Dad pulled the two bowls closer to the wok.

"This important time. Add meat back now. Watch 'til everything hot and then add sauce but be sure to slide down the side of wok heat it up before touch food."

The color and consistency of the sauce changed, turning into a glaze as it began to cover the ingredients.

"This tricky part. Go slower better than faster. Use finger like this blend cornstarch with water. No lumps. See. Drop little by little. Watch sauce thicken, but too much and the sauce turns to glue. No good. Less better."

It was a chemistry lesson in action. It was a culinary feast for my eyes that matched the flavors of every morsel cooked to perfection. "No matter what you cook. Same same."

I wasn't surprised when Dad's spirit joined me in the kitchen. He was delighted when I'd mastered Shrimp with Honey Sauce and Caramelized Walnuts. His eyes lit up when I added my twist to a recipe, like the time I made a sweet and sour sauce for lettuce wraps but added some hoisin sauce at the end to give it an extra zing.

It was rewarding to master cooking, but it was even more rewarding when I discovered the way to travel to my father's homeland.

***

I was surprised when he peeked over my shoulder as I typed in a word for a Google search. Dad didn't use a computer, but he seemed fascinated. The Internet made looking things up a lot easier for me, words like Qing Ming and Chung Yeung and hungry ghost.

Sometimes, I'd wake up with a phrase in my thoughts, words I knew Dad wanted me to find. Late in 2015, I woke up with the words "San Duo" niggling at the back of my mind as if pushing me to the iPad. By now, I was familiar with the name of the village where my father was born in China. How many times had I tried to locate the village?

My problem was that I knew approximately where the village was but not definitely, and China is a huge place. I tried to wrap my mind around the size and population of Taishan County. Taishan County, a 1267.70 square mile area, is four times the size where I currently live (307 square miles when you combined the city of Richmond and Henrico County). Taishan's population was 941,095 in 2010, while Richmond/Henrico combined was only 545,444.

When I scrolled down through the results, a name caught my attention: Roots Program - Friends of Roots. A click and I felt as if cymbals clanged.

My heartbeat quickened as I typed "Louie" into the search line at the Friends of Roots village database and our surname and the district and village popped up on the screen. Dad stood by me and smiled. "That my home. You want know my home. Go there."

When everything checked out, I contacted the Roots people. I do not speak Chinese, so I needed someone I could trust to help me communicate as well as find my way around in China. John Wong told me that the Friends of Roots team works with people at the Guangdong Overseas Chinese Vocational School, who do the fieldwork in Guangdong Province. Most of the early Chinese who ventured to the United States were from this province. I knew so little about my ancestors and ancestral village, but I felt I had to take this next step wherever it guided me. China drew me like a magnetic force.

I planned a trip to California. I requested information from the National Archives and Records Administration (NARA) in San Bruno. I hoped to be able to examine files about my father's and uncle's journey from China to the U.S. That was another hurdle because I did not have very much information and later found out that some of the information I had was incorrect or incomplete. However, my ancestors were watching over me because when I did arrive for my appointment at NARA, the research archivist Gloria said she found my father's and uncle's files and another file for a "Louie Mow."

"I don't know a Louie Mow," I said to her, but took the file and put it to the side while I perused my father's file. I held the "Heading for Testimony" documents in my hands and read "In the matter of Louie Hung On, Son of Merchant," and then I devoured the next twenty-one pages as if they were the hottest best-seller off the press. Page one stated that Louie Mow was the "alleged father" of Louie Hung On. I saw the photos of Dad as a kid and of his father and Louie Mow's brother, Louie Kaow.

I quickly grabbed the file I'd put aside and began to dig through it like an archaeologist dusting the dirt off an ancient bone with a horsehair brush. I discovered more photos and more names of people and places as I gently turned the document pages in the files. The image of my father immigrating to San Francisco as a cook changed before my eyes into a young man groomed into a long line of successful merchants. Careful not to let my tears fall on the papers from the archives, I dabbed the wet streams that flowed uncontrollably. If there had been any doubt that I was ready to make this voyage, they melted away as I wept for joy.

"Thank you, Grandfather," I said knowing he was helping me just as surely as if he were standing over my shoulder. "Louie Mow, Louie Hong Wei, my grandfather," I whispered reverently.

Although I'd never met him, I felt so close to him in that moment and knew he'd guide me to the ancestral village I had longed to see.

In the meantime, I copied files and asked for the one for my great-grandfather, Louie Fat, the forty-three-year-old Grant Avenue merchant who testified in February 1907 on behalf of his son's (Louie Mow) arrival.

In October, I headed back to California for more research at NARA before leaving for China on October 29. I had corresponded with Charles Miller, who found and sent me copies of the Partners Lists in the business records, but I wanted to see the actual files. I was surprised when I met fellow researchers who, as it turned out, were also searching for information about their Louie ancestors. We compared notes and found the same names in both files and knew there was a connection between our families. (As of this writing, we have connected more dots – like the fact that our family's villages were within walking distance of each other - but have not yet found our common ancestor.)

Certain that my rooting adventure was more than about my genealogy, I wrestled with the question of whether I would dishonor our family if I told the truth. My search for understanding to heal the past of this lifetime led me to a previous life with my present mother and father.

I knew that coming to grips with truth in this lifetime would affect the future, and this time Dad did not wave his hand in the air at me saying, "Be American." Meaning "Don't go there."

"You don't have to say anything now if you don't want to," I said to Dad's ghost, "but at a point in time, we must face everything we've ever done, atone for everything, every thought, word, and action." After the experience in the Tenth Hell, he understood me and that I held no animosity toward him.

Conversing with a ghost has its quirks. For one thing, sometimes the communication is like watching a movie, but with commentary to fill in whatever gaps of understanding. It is as if someone knows the questions I think as I view the video and feeds me the answers. I'd know things about the scene because of the research for my roots, but then I'd catch myself thinking "Where did that come from or how did I know that?" I felt as if we had melded our minds until there were times when I had difficulty knowing where my point of view stopped, and theirs' began.

Every medium has his/her unique way of working, but this is the way it works for me. Sometimes when I wake up in the morning, I know I am still in a hypnagogic state, the experience of the transition from wakefulness to sleep.

Other times, for instance, when I meditate, I slip into that state of consciousness. I sense that I have one foot in the spirit world and one foot in the physical world.

Often, when I know a ghost is around, I ask "What do you want to say?" When he/she is ready to talk to me, I get a feeling like opening a program on the computer; how it makes a sound indicating that the program is turning on. Instead of sounds, I get a *knowing* that the channel is on. I am then ready to either speak or to allow automatic writing to happen and record what they say or show me.

Automatic writing is a form of channeling, allowing communication to come to me from the other side. The laws of the spirit world are different than those in the physical world. Therefore, communication that seems to stop and start over a period of days, weeks, or months for me is as if no time has elapsed on the other side. It can be frustrating, but I listen, record, and file the information until I have enough to see the bigger picture. Sometimes, the information comes so quickly that it is all I can do to write it down before I lose the connection.

For instance, when Dad showed me a replay of his life, I saw the visitors' area at Angel Island, a detention center for immigrants off the coast of San Francisco from 1910-1940. It is no Ellis Island and its inhabitants experienced a different standard of treatment.

My grandfather Louie Mow came to see his seventeen-year-old son, Louie Hung On, after he arrived in the U.S. for the first time in January of 1928.

Dad showed me where his distrust for white people and the U.S. began, why he wanted to protect me from the prejudice he'd experienced. Why he had insisted that I "Be American."

***

"Bàbà, why I no go with you?" Louie Hung On asked his father. He felt exhausted from the voyage on the S. S. President Jackson. It was the longest trip he'd ever made away from home. There were other members of the Louie clan on board, but Louie Hung On longed to be with his father instead of detained on Angel Island. He knew something was amiss. He didn't have to understand English to know that there was a problem. He heard something different in the doctor's tone of voice. "Baba, I did what the doctor told me to do. I shit in the pot."

Louie Mow searched his son's eyes and patted his shoulder, "I know, son. They tested it, and there a problem. Eggs of liver worm."

Fear gripped Louie Hung On like a vise. The fear he'd be turned back, shame that he'd dishonor his family, but his father reassured him, "Just delay. Doctor treat. Shit again. Test again. Worm gone."

Louie Hung On's shoulders curled. He could not hide his disappointment, so he lowered his head in submission. "But I come soon?" he asked, "Worm go away. Then, I come big city with you?"

"Yes, son. Be patient. You come soon," Louie Mow said. He was disappointed too. After all that he had done to pre-register his son for admission into the U.S., Louie Mow was also relieved that he did not bring his son a few years earlier when a diagnosis of the liver worm, or Chinese liver fluke as the white man called it, would have meant immediate rejection. Louie Mow had read the accounts of Zhonghua's wife in the Chinese newspapers. It was big news. He heard about Dr. Fred Lam, who convinced the surgeon general to reclassify clonorchiasis as a treatable disease that should not prevent someone from entering the U.S.

Louie Mow asked Mr. G.T. Marsh about what the American papers said about the case whenever they met at the store to trade some curios (Chinese and Japanese merchandise). "Why so hard on Chinaman?" he'd asked, "No treat same as other man."

Mr. Marsh said, "Some people are just plain ignorant or do not appreciate China's long history. They do not know how advanced a civilization China is, nor all the inventions created in China while the Western world slumbered. This attitude will change in time, but for now, we will find a way around the politics of the day."

Marsh had a profound love for Asia ever since his trip from Australia to San Francisco by way of Japan in 1872, a trip that set into motion his life's passion for Asian art objects.

He liked Louie Mow and his father Louie Fat, whom he'd known for years. They helped him rebuild his inventory after the 1906 earthquake destroyed his shop inside the Palace Hotel on Market Street. Was it so long ago?

Marsh thought about Louie Mow's arrival in February of 1907, less than a year after the earthquake. He observed the handsome lad at Louie's shop on Bush Street, where they met to conduct business while he waited for the re-building of the Palace Hotel.

Louie Fat assured him that Fong Sang Lung & Co., later known as Wah Sang Lung & Co., could sell Marsh whatever he needed to start up again at a fair price, because Louie Fat was indebted to Marsh for all the times he'd stood up for the Louie family. Louie Fat knew his connection with Marsh carried weight with the immigration officials. However, if not for the Zhonghua case, the U.S. Public Health Service would still exclude potential immigrants infected with the Chinese liver fluke. Louie Hung On's prospects in 1928 would have been very different, but fate was on his side.

Once cleared through immigration, lessons at the Baptist Mission School at 15 Waverly Place filled Louie Hung On's days and more lessons at the Chinese Salvation Army School at the corner of Waverly and Sacramento filled his nights. Both schools were near the Wah Sang Lung & Co. store on Grant Avenue where his father and grandfather were partners.

Louie Hung On walked the streets of San Francisco's Chinatown alone, stopped at the shop to grab a bite to eat, help with the chores, and crawl into his pallet on a shelf in the basement of the store at the end of the day.

In 1930, it was time to follow another family tradition. Louie Hung On went back to China to start a family, and with any luck, his first child would be a son. Looking out the window of the steamship as it pulled out of San Francisco Bay, he thought about his family. "Wait until my brothers hear about Gam Saan, about the gifts I carry for Māma." He smiled with pride as he held the gold bracelet for his wife. He was married before he left China in 1928, but he returned to San Francisco without a chance to know his bride. Lee Yook Moi, whose chart aligned with his, was a perfect match. Lee Yook Moi, who came from Ling Gong village, settled into the Louie household and quickly learned what pleased her mother-in-law. "Now, I will have some time know my wife."

Following in the footsteps of his father and his father's father, Louie Hong On did what his family expected of him as the first-born son. He consummated his marriage, and when his wife was into her last term of her pregnancy, Louie Hong On returned to San Francisco.

China was going through changes of her own. The Chinese Revolution overthrew the last Ching Emperor, who became the monarch two years before Louie Hung On was born. Chaos ruled the homeland.

The family's best chance was to amass whatever fortune they could in the U.S. and prepare for the worst.

Meanwhile, in China, Lee Yook Moi gave birth to a son, but she died soon afterward. Another red thread of fate ripped apart on the tapestry of our tree of life. Our grandfather named his first grandson Do-Young, which meant "raised by his grandparents." With the change of circumstances in China, the tradition of sending the eldest son to the Gold Mountain broke down and Do-Young did not meet his father until many years later.

***

Dad's ghost told me stories as mesmerizing as those told by Scheherazade, but I longed for more. Connecting with the Friends of Roots group gave me a glimmer of hope that I would finally find San Duo and that I'd be able to communicate with the villagers through my guides. I knew that I must take a leap of faith before it was too late.

"Before they're gone," Dad said, but I had no idea what he meant until I made the trip to China. It was magical how things started to fall into place once I made the commitment.

October 29, 2016, arrived. I recognized other Rooters gathering at the San Francisco Airport and knew that in twenty-three hours, we would begin the journey of a lifetime in our ancestors' homeland.

On the warm South China morning of November 3rd, we went to Debbie Anderson's village, stopped for lunch, and then, it was my turn.

We did not go very far when the bus pulled over to the side of the highway, and my fellow rooters, guides, and I stepped off the bus. Instead of a fancy entrance like the ones we found on the previous days, we found an old street sign marking Sam Dor/San Duo village 三多村. I held onto that signpost to steady myself and said, "I'm finally here. I'm finally here."

We walked down the street into the village fronted by a factory instead of ponds and fields as in the other villages. Piles of debris and construction supplies sat on our right, newly built houses and houses in construction stood on our left; an old woman holding onto her walking stick in one hand as she sat with her other hand resting on the arm of a pink plastic chair watched over both. Our guides approached her and asked her if she was the eldest person in the village. Dad left San Duo almost one hundred years ago, so my hope of finding someone who knew him was slim, but I hoped that a descendent of previous generations of the Louie clan might give us some validation of the records I'd found at NARA. Could she be such a descendent? I listened patiently and tried to pick up any clues, and even though I did not understand what they said, I sensed that things were not going well until I heard one of the guides say, "She's saying something about three sons."

"My grandfather had two brothers," I said, "but my father had five brothers and one sister."

I named Dad's brothers off hoping their names would trigger her memory. It wasn't until much later that I realized that Dad and two of his brothers were born in San Duo, but the other brothers were born in Gung Yick.

More conversations with the lady with the pink chair and her elderly friend who looked as if she did not know what to make of our entourage, and then we headed to a house. It was like the other five-room houses we had seen in other villages, although a decoratively pierced partition under the altar loft subdivided the parlor into two sections. However, an inspection of the family tablets on the altar dashed any hopes that the house belonged to my family. After climbing the ladder to the loft and peering around the room, I felt claustrophobic and had to get out of the house.

Remembering the diagram that I'd made from the descriptions in the immigration files, I pulled it out and retraced my tracks back to the beginning of the village. It was confusing because I did not know if the new buildings I saw when we entered the village were renovated structures or built in front of the old ones.

I walked back out to the street and oriented myself to the head and tail of the village described by my grandfather. The tail was to the left/West, and the head was to the right/East.

I walked toward the left and asked my ancestors to guide me as they did before when I looked for Uncle Don's gravesite. Second row, second and fourth houses. However, when I walked toward the second row, I saw a vacant lot where a tractor sat like a watchdog. I intended to walk beyond the lot, but an invisible force stopped me, and as I tried to back up, it pushed me from behind. My guide Elsie followed me but from a safe distance.

"Okay. I get it. You're trying to show me something, but I do not understand. What are you trying to show me?"

I heard the words "Gung Yick."

"Okay. I understand. Go to Gung Yick."

The rest of the group caught up with me and said that we were going to go on to the next village, Hong May, which was a few miles away.

"How far is it to Gung Yick?" I asked as we piled back on the bus and headed north. When we drove into the village, a large pond and fields sat peacefully to the right of the paved driveway and houses – old and new – dotted the left side. Drying rice strewn the pavement between the pond and the houses as if promising grains of clues about to be given up to us. We disembarked the bus again, and 雷荣仰 Lei Rong Yang, the village chief (Lei is the Putonghua/modern Chinese form of Louie), greeted us.

After many conversations with my guides, he led us to my great-grandfather's property. Since Mr. Lei was young, I asked Walter to ask him if he knew my half-brother, Do-Yeany, who did not leave China until the late 1970's. He recognized the name and said that he saw Do-Yeany a few years back when they went to the gravesites for Ching Ming. Do-Yeany's mother, Lee Yook Moi, was related to his family. Mr. Lei said he knew where she burial site and could take us there, but it was two hours away.

We arrived at our destination, but there was no house, just an overgrown lot dotted with yellow blossomed plants. "This is the place," Albert said, "where your great-grandfather's house was but it was torn down a long time ago. This is all that is left."

Narrow alleyways less than four feet wide surrounded the lot where the house once stood. An open drain hugged one side of the walkway. Black mold covered the gray brick of the neighbor's home, which would have butted my family's home. The mold revealed an outline of the previous structure, lower in the front of the building facing South and higher in the back.

The building to the North was different from the others. It was much smaller and had an inner courtyard. Stucco painted white covered the brick.

A senior woman peeked out occasionally but ducked back into her tiny house whenever anyone looked her way. Her little house tucked amid the taller structures felt inviting. Had she planted the lot in front of her house with the yellow blossoming vines?

My great-grandfather's home was probably built in the 1800's in typical gray brick fashion. It probably had five rooms, two kitchens – one on the front and another on the back near the doors, two bedrooms and a main parlor in the middle, where a loft would have held the family altar and acted as a storage space. Small windows must have dotted the walls on three sides to allow circulation such as it could be in such tight quarters. The tile floor would have felt cool in the hottest days of the year. To the left of the parlor, a wood seating platform called a kang would have been the central piece of furniture in the room. Used for seating, dining, and writing by day with a short table placed on it, the kang converted to a bed by night with the table removed. Depending on the family's wealth, other tables and stools would have graced the room, and scrolls or paintings adorned the walls.

As merchants of "fancy goods," I wondered if any of the furniture, porcelain, or silks they traded made their way into their homes.

Nowadays, the villagers pulled up folding plywood tables and plastic stools to meet their needs. In some of the other homes, we saw paintings or portraits of the ancestors prominently placed on the walls, a custom from long ago still carried on.

I walked out into the center of the lot to feel its energy. Sunshine warmed my body and soul as I closed my eyes, and feeling more centered as I breathed deeply, I asked, "Grandfather, are you here? Tell me what to do." Suddenly, I felt lost in a surreal dimension.

***

Zit, zit, zit, a sound like a 3-D printer whirled around me, and the walls of the house appeared. Joy filled the air, red eggs graced the blue and white porcelain bowl on the table, and a beautiful scroll announced the birth of a son named Louie Fat 雷發.

Dressed in an orchid silk gown with delicate embroidery of lotus blossoms and butterflies, his mother wobbled as she adjusted her bound feet on the tile floors. She knew her son's destiny was to travel across the ocean on a big ship many times and to live in the barbarian's world.

***

Just as suddenly, the vision disappeared, and I stood in the middle of the vacant lot. "Good. Now I am ready."

Although there were no altars as in the other homes, I created my own on the ground with rocks stacked to hold the incense, and most of all, my Uncle Don's poem, which I repeated like a mantra calling the spirits of my ancestors to me. I felt the men of my family gather around me, my uncle stands next to me, and places his hand on my right shoulder as I said the last line, "Within knowledge can be found literary talents."

"You have come home. Will you tell our story?" Uncle Don said.

"Yes! Yes! It's time to tell the story." I was so glad to bring his poem to his homeland even though he died an old bachelor in a distant county.

I made an altar for the women in the rear of the house near the kitchen. "I know you're here with me also. I know how strong you were to stay behind and take care of things at home. I feel your strength in me, and now I know that I also share another gift from you, great-great-grandmother. I know that I was in this family in another life. I know it." I felt the women stand a little taller, grateful that I recognized their contribution to the family. I sensed that they knew who I was even though we had never met in this life.

When I completed the rituals, I said to Walter, "This was perfect."

What happened next and at dinner was even more perfect. The altered state I had entered during my meditation at the lot prepared me for three remarkable events I knew were affirmations about moving forward with my dharma, my life purpose.

I gave the village chief a red basket with lai see, a red envelope with money inside, but I also wanted to give him a hug in gratitude for his help. Knowing that the Louie clan was not an affectionate group of people, I asked Walter to ask the village leader if it would be okay for me to give him a hug. Walter translated my question and replied, "It's okay," but when I reached out to hug the chief, he extended his hand. Not sure if it was a translation issue or as I suspected, I respectfully shook his hand, and then another vision flashed in my mind's eye. Understanding what happened, I turned to Walter, "Ask him if it's okay if I read his palm." This time, the chief extended his hand with a smile on his face. Chinese like fortune tellers.

"You've seen many changes in your lifetime, and you've had to be strong for others," I said, "but it is important for you also to allow yourself to feel your feelings. At the very least, do not hide them from yourself or you create a wall around you that blocks good things coming to you." He laughed and walked away towards the alleyway to the North.

Was that a message for him, or was it for me, or was it for both of us?

Albert noticed that the chief held a water pipe in his hands and told me to go and check it out. He showed me how to use it. He pressed a few leaves of tobacco into a slit in the bamboo and lit them. A gurgling sound echoed inside the bamboo pipe, and smoke floated out of the village chief's nostrils as a wide grin showed off his toothy smile, and for a moment, we bonded.

Mr. Yang, the head of the Overseas Chinese office who was our local official guide, pulled me to the side alley. I thought I was in trouble because Mr. Yang was stern. Albert had warned us that whenever Mr. Yang said anything, we had to pay attention. When he said that it was time to go, we headed directly for the bus like obedient school children. Something was different in his tone. He spoke to me as if I understood, but fortunately, Albert was close by and translated for me. Moved by the ceremony to honor my ancestors, Mr. Yang told me he believed in the spirits who were with me.

Before we left the lot, a woman from the village brought out a tray with pastries, and in traditional fashion, we ended this part of the rituals with a sweet taste in our mouths. When we joined the other Rooters, we discovered the source of the pastries. The village women who gathered in the community center made the delicacies for a wedding that was to take place in three days.

Now I understood why I made so many crocheted baskets. Although we had encountered only a few people at the place where my great-grandfather's house stood, I dispensed the rest of the baskets to the ladies and included a special lai see for the bride-to-be to wish her prosperity for her marriage. I wondered if she and her husband would be there when I return in the future or if she would be married off to another village as was the custom in the old days. Even though we only found an empty lot, meeting the women of the village preparing for a celebration was the perfect ending for the day, but it got better.

As my fellow rooters loaded the bus, I noticed Mr. Yang hung back talking to Walter. Walter said, "He wants you to read his hand." Without hesitating or even thinking about this important official asking me to give him a reading, I took a breath and asked my ancestors to show me a message for Mr. Yang. At first, I felt some resistance, but then he began to open his energies, and suddenly I saw what I needed to share.

"You have so much responsibility that you sometimes forget to ask for help, but it is important to allow others to help you, and when you do this, *magic will happen.*" I knew that message well because I was once the same, and I knew the magical things that happened when I allowed the Universe to help me on my journey.

I knew this principle was what made this trip a reality for me. I sensed that Mr. Yang needed the confirmation of seeing the spirits, of affirming his need to be more open, and I wondered what wonderful things were in store for him, but I also knew to let go because everything would happen in his divine order.

Everyone noticed a change in Mr. Yang after we left my village. Several people commented to me later how his energy softened, and he seemed much more relaxed the rest of the day. The magic was beginning.

Cindy, one of our guides from the Guangdong Overseas Chinese Vocational School, must have noticed it too because she asked me at dinner what was it that I did at the village when I held the chief's and Mr. Yang's hands. I tried to explain to her that I have a gift for seeing things and the hand is one way for me to connect with a person's energy. "It's called psychometry," I said, "but here, let me show you. I studied palmistry when I was younger but didn't practice it enough, so I forgot what the lines meant. However, whenever I held someone's hands, the lines seemed to talk to me, sometimes even contradicting what I remembered they were supposed to indicate."

"What do you see in my hands?" she said.

I could feel her openness as I held her right hand, and a scene moved quickly across my mind. I had to replay it like rewinding a movie and reviewing it again.

I even slowed down the motion, so I could see the scenes more clearly, but I was not sure if I could share with Cindy what I saw yet, so I asked for her left hand.

The right hand speaks to me about the present and the future, but the left hand speaks to me about the past, especially about past lives. What I saw in the left hand confirmed what I knew from the scenes that played and replayed in my mind as if to get my attention.

I saw Cindy in a past life as a man in Japan, a warrior who fought dutifully for a Samurai, but when the Samurai asked for an opinion about a warfare tactic he was considering, the man spoke truthfully from his years of experience. However, the Samurai took the man's advice as a criticism and without hesitation whacked off his head.

It should not have surprised me. My specialty is past lives, and I knew we change genders and nationalities from one lifetime to the next. Still, I searched for the words to tell Cindy what I saw knowing that Chinese and Japanese relationships could still trigger people.

"Do you have neck problems, Cindy?" I began. "And do you also have challenges speaking up to your superiors?"

"Oh, yes. I get a pain in the back of my neck all the time, but I always follow my superiors' orders," she said.

"Let me explain a little bit more about what I do. Besides talking with ghosts, I see the spirits of people's past lives. I am a Past Life Regression Therapist and help people heal the past, so they can be happier in the present and create a better future," I said unsure if Cindy believed in reincarnation or not.

I realized that the Chinese were much more open to talking about certain subjects than when I was there in 1985, but I had not had a personal conversation with Cindy to know what her beliefs were. Trusting that if I saw the past life, she must be more open than I realized, I continued, "What I saw was that in a previous life, you were a man in Japan. You were a warrior who fought many years for a Samurai and for his son, who also became Samurai. One day the younger Samurai asked for an opinion about a warfare tactic. You explained to him the drawbacks of such a maneuver. You spoke truthfully from your years of experience. However, the Samurai took your advice as an affront. He impulsively drew his sword and whacked off your head."

Cindy winced as she took in the imagery, but she never questioned being a man in another lifetime, nor in being Japanese.

"Is it okay if I put my hand on the back of your neck and draw out the residual energy left there by the memory of what happened in that lifetime?"

She nodded. When I placed my right hand on her neck and my left hand on her right shoulder to steady her body, she began to cry. Twenty or so people surrounded us in the private dining room, but it was as if only Cindy and I were in the space. I put my arms around her and then I felt a presence surround us and merge with my body. Cindy sobbed, and I hugged her close to me. "Everything's okay. Everything's okay," I said as a scene from the movie Ghost appeared in my mind's eye.

Cindy said, "I felt my mother's embrace when you touched me. My mother has been dead for four years, and I miss her."

"I know," I said, "she wanted to give you a hug and to reassure you that she is okay, and you are okay and that she loves you very much." I did not know if Cindy saw the movie Ghost, the scene where Patrick Swayze's character entered Whoopi Goldberg's body to give Demi Moore's character one last hug before he went to the other side, but I could tell that she understood.

Then, another scene flashed on the screen of my inner eye. This one was of two monks at the Shaolin Temple. I knew that was why Cindy and I had a strong connection. We were those monks in yet another lifetime.

"Cindy, I believe you can do the same kind of work that I do, to see things, to know things, which will help people," I said.

I know you have a small child now, and that is where you need to focus your attention, but stay aware, and when the time is right you will be guided. It took me a long time to accept these gifts. I was older than you are now, but when I did, my life changed dramatically and for the better." This time we hugged, and tears of joy filled our eyes. I knew that this was one of those magical moments I had told Mr. Yang about and that the "red thread of fate" had pulled and tugged at Cindy and me, bringing us together again. It was a perfect ending to a day that started out with one hurdle after another.

My quest was both ending and beginning. I knew that I would come back again.

Afterword

STILL SEEKING TRUTH

2017
Richmond, Virginia

It has taken twenty-five years to write this story. There are still many mysteries. The story will never be complete, but that's okay. I realize that for me writing is a "living meditation."

I began by wanting to document my father's funeral for my family. It felt important to record, and hopefully, shed some light on the Buddhist rituals for my Amer-Asian family as well as for my Chinese American family who was raised in Communist China.

When I finished the story about Dad's funeral and sent it to my family, Wai Gauy said, "The story is not finished." I did not know then how true his statement was, but from that moment, the story took on a life of its own.

As I wind up this chapter, I have many unanswered questions, for with every answer that I did discover more questions popped into my mind.

For instance, a new document from NARA gave me my great-great-grandfather's name, more pieces of the puzzle. I believe it is a never-ending story. Even as I search for my answers, I embrace the ambiguity.

What have I learned from my conversations with Dad's ghost? First, love transcends time and space and physical existence because there is no death. The physical body may die, but something greater lives on. Secondly, what goes around comes around. Thirdly, I am only responsible for myself because I only have control over *my* thoughts and actions.

Therefore, although I have asked Dad why he has not asked forgiveness from my mother, I have no control over his choices. Dad has made progress on the other side since we began our conversations but now, he must test what he has learned in the spirit world and act from his conscious awareness in the physical world. It's the same principle as putting into practice in the real world what you learn in school. He will choose a life that will give him the right opportunities. Will he choose the other-side-of-the-coin or will he choose a life of service? In other words, will he decide to be reborn as a female into an abusive situation? Or will he dedicate his next life to protect women and children from abuse?

Likewise, I do not have control over my mother's choices. She did not say "I'm sorry I did not protect you and help you more. I am sorry I was so hard on you, taking my frustrations out on you." before she died, but I now understand the consequences of her actions, of both my parent's actions, without being attached to them.

I understand the meaning of compassion and unconditional love. They must choose their way just as I have chosen mine. We are all subject to the Laws of Karma and will meet the consequences of our decisions in Divine Order.

My life is much different than it was twenty-seven years ago, because I chose the path of love and forgiveness. I have a better understanding of who I am and of my purpose in this life and my journey on this planet.

As I explore the bigger picture, I realize that this life is but a blip in eternity. The other ghosts continue to show me more blips, but that's another story.

About the Author

Carole Louie's spiritual journey began in earnest when she overcame her lifelong fear of ghosts to communicate with her father's spirit and her world turned inside out.

An award-winning Interior Designer, Louie juggled the experiences of her spiritual journey with the mundane world. Conversations with her father's ghost helped her accept her gift as a medium. Her explorations into her father's Buddhist beliefs about ghosts and reincarnation inspired her to delve into the teachings of reincarnation. Her next book shares stories from her memories of ten past lives and reincarnation research.

Louie studied relaxation response, guided imagery, and music and meditation with Joseph Spano, M.D. and meditation and channeling with Sanaya Roman.

Certified in Past Life Regression Therapy with The Weiss Institute and Carol Bowman, Louie incorporates her gifts as a medium with her PLRT sessions to empower you to heal, transform, and grow spiritually.

Louie founded THE CENTER-RVA, a center for spiritual growth in Richmond, VA, to empower others on their spiritual path.

Learn more about Carole and explore the *Conversations* Gallery

at **www.carolelouie.com**

Learn more about THE CENTER-RVA at

www.thecenter-rva.com

Other Stories by Carole Louie

The Legacy of the Lei Family Architects Lives On: The Story of Yangshi Lei is a continuation of Carole's genealogy research that led her to the gates of the Forbidden City and to the architects who built one fifth of China's World Heritage Sites.

The Not So Secret Life of Emily Elizabeth is a paranormal mystery, cozy fiction based on memories of a past life.

The short story, *I Remember*, one of fourteen stories collected from around the world by Rabbi Yonassan Gershom, is featured in the anthology *From Ashes to Healing: Mystical Encounters with the Holocaust.*

Grounding is a meditation in *Meditations for Awakening* edited by Larry Moen.

CAROLE LOUIE

Acknowledgements

Twenty-odd years ago, I never would have guessed that I would owe a debt of gratitude to the ghosts/spirits in my life. They have helped me see the world in a new way, and I am grateful for their guidance.

Dad's spirit was my first guide to the other side. The conversations with him and witnessing his experience "on the other side," have taught me the meaning of 孝顺 xiàoshun (filial piety). When I struggled with telling the dark side of his story, he said, "Must tell truth. Must do what is right." Although I never met his father, Louie Mow, and his grandfather, Louie Fat, I know my grandfather and great-grandfather have guided me back to China. I believe they knew my connection to China was deeper than our genes. My maternal grandmother was the first to acknowledge my ability to see ghosts and her spirit urged me to tell my story for my daughter and grandchildren as a legacy greater than anything else I could give them. Mom, who died in January of 2016, did not waste any time pushing me forward to make the trip to China knowing I needed to go there to finish my story.

Many people on this side of the veil helped me birth this book through their encouragement and expertise. Thanks to Cheryl Pallant for her gift as a mentor to help me develop my craft as a writer. I am grateful to Pat Concordora who helped me with editing. Any mistakes I missed are my own. Thank you to Susan Hughes who taught me to honor the *perfection of imperfections* in this process. I am grateful to the folks at CreateSpace who made self-publishing easier to share my story and to edit it as the story evolves.

I am grateful to Sanaya Roman and Joe Spano, M.D. for helping me create a foundation for my spiritual growth through meditation practices. I am grateful to Arthur Cataldo, Brian Weiss, M.D., Carole Weiss, and Carol Bowman—my Past Life Regression Therapy teachers—for guiding me through processes that helped me transcend the past.

Thank you to my Chinese School teachers who have taught me how to say my Chinese name, to translate my Zupu (family genealogy book), and to speak better Chinese than when I began this story. I am grateful to Ying Liu at the William and Mary Confucius Institute who has inspired me to dig deeper for more ancestral roots and to write a story that will be in my next book. It is a story that will weave together my fascination with my ancestry, my love of the Chinese culture, and my love of architecture through many lifetimes.

I have learned about the Chinese traditions of defining family; however, the definition of "family" has grown for me. I am grateful for the reunion of my sisters from previous lives— Pat Eaton, Donna Fuller, and Terri McDowell—and to my sister Florence who have encouraged me to "go confidently in the direction of my dreams." I am grateful to all the soul brothers and sisters I have met through the creation of this book.

I am eternally grateful to my daughter Jennie for everything, including Jake and Marisa. This book is my way to tell you how much I love you. I hope you know that I am doing the best I can, that I am a *work-in-progress*. I am grateful for our reunion in this life.

I would also like to thank Tim Scanlan and Celia Tuttle, who helped me in the beginning stages, and to Friends of Roots, the folks at NARA, who helped me with the last stage—my trip to China. I have shared this journey with many family members, friends, clients, and fellow Rooters who inspire me with their questions.

I believe you have found this book for a reason. Even though I do not know you, I am sure you are on a spiritual path. How do I know this? It's easy. Something—an inexplicable something— has brought you to this book. If you've made it this far, remember this: whether you believe my story or not right now, you cannot erase it from your mind. *You cannot unring the bell.*

The knowledge of my experiences might be as tiny as a mustard seed dropped into the newly tilled soil, or as mighty as Thor's hammer breaking down walls you've built around yourself.

You can pick parts of it to savor and reject other parts as if you're at a Super King Buffet. You can ruminate on it and spit out whatever you cannot digest.

The point is you are a being of free will. Therefore, you can choose what to believe about my story or not.

More importantly, you can choose how to live your life every step of the way. Life is a process as well as a journey. Remember, to bring love into the process. I honor you and the path you choose because I know your path and mine connect us by a red thread of fate.

One Last Thing…

Conversations is a "living meditation." Like the spaces between the letters and lines, my story has an energy beyond its words. Sit with it, ruminate on it, and feel what is right for you. Notice when you read my story if you experienced goose bumps those tell-tale signals from someone on the other side.

I would love to hear your reactions, your questions, and comments. Contact me at carolelouie5555@gmail.com.

If you enjoyed this book or found it useful, I would be very grateful if you would post a brief review on Amazon. Your support does make a difference, and I read all the reviews personally.

Thanks again for your support!

Printed in Great Britain
by Amazon

48762058R00096